RAH RAH AND ROOS BACKPACKING AUSTRALIA

Farming and Travel in the Great Southern Land

Stephen Malins

DISCLAIMER

All names have been changed and there are characters who are composites of more than one person. Some places and dates have been changed.

CONTENTS

Departing Busselton Field, Western Australia

DEDICATION

To my brother, Jez, who went when he was called

PROLOGUE

*400 miles from Sydney, New
South Wales, Australia*

New South Wales, Australia, 2002.

I'm in the passenger seat of a Toyota Land Cruiser. Glen is driving. He's a 6' 4" redhead. He's wearing a tatty, wide-brimmed farmers' Akubra hat, and maintains a beard, which I'm guessing provides protection from the sun. My hat is in my lap, which I've had the sense to knock around a bit, so it's not quite so new looking. The last thing I need is to look like the "new boy".

We're skimming the dirt road corrugations at 60 mph. Glen steers with one hand, and holds a stubbie of Toohey's New beer in the other. He takes sips occasionally, and glances at me.

Looking through the fly-encrusted windscreen, I can see the bleak countryside is barren. There is a drought in this part of New South Wales, and the ground is cracked and arid. The sun is kissing the horizon, so twilight will follow soon.

Two silhouettes flit across the road in front, and I crane forward to see. Glen has barely time to react, but flicks the Toyota to the side of the road and misses one shape, but I feel a thud as we strike the second with the bull bar. I am puzzled momentarily; then it dawns on me. Kangaroos!

"You miss the first, you always hit the second," he explains.

I grin inanely, and nod, enlightened with this local knowledge —it all seems very exciting, if alarming. The CB radio crackles into life, and he wedges his stubbie in his lap and reaches for the mike on the dash.

"You on channel, Glen?" A woman's voice.

"Yup," he replies.

"You on your way back?"

"Back home in ten minutes, Bronnie."

"Is Steve with you?"

"Yup."

"See ya later. Dinner will be ready."

So this is farm life. I've been challenged before.

*Ten years before: 800ft or so above
ground-level, Oxfordshire, England*

1 992. For the last 15 minutes, I have been in agony. The combined weight of my parachute, reserve, 5.56mm rifle and pack, some 55kg, is causing my arm and hand, which is grasping the strop hooked to the overhead static line, to go numb.

Looking around, I can see that I'm not the only one in a private world of misery. Men next to me are grumbling and sweating, trying to shift the weight of their equipment on to the sides of the C-130 Hercules transport plane which is flying low level, minutes away from the Drop Zone. The side doors are open, so the noise is a din. It is dark in the plane, but the autumnal sunshine leaks in.

At least I am not "Number One". Last time we jumped, I stood transfixed with fear in the door looking at the fuel tank on the wing, trying not to look down. There was no real sense of height: in fact, the ground looked alarmingly close. The slipstream outside was tugging at my legs, rippling my trousers, so two crouching RAF jumpmasters had got hold of my waist, one squinting under my arm watching for the green light.

I am jolted back to the present by a barely audible shout:

"Red On!"—a few seconds tick by:

"Green on–GO!"

Adrenaline levels go through the roof.

I shuffle in step to the door, lugging my gear. Nothing can stop a plane full of paras exiting a plane with two men jumping from both sides of the aircraft at half-second intervals. 90 men are gone in 45 seconds. The dispatchers are trying to regulate the flow—each loaded man steadied briefly at the door before being launched—but we want out, with some flopping out, disappearing from view in an instant.

I don't remember jumping: one moment I am approaching the door, the next I'm in the slipstream. It's like standing in a gigantic blast furnace. I have exited with my legs apart, so I feel myself spiral down the side of the aircraft twisting my rigging lines as my 'chute streams out behind me. My parachute finishes developing above me and everything is quiet—for what seems like the first time in hours.

Blessed relief.

In the sudden brightness, I get glimpses of Oxfordshire, but we're not here for the view. I am aware of shouts in the air around me, and heavier men are below. I kick out of the twists, nerves rising. Others are close, so I grab a handful of rigging lines and steer away into my own airspace—the last thing I want right now is an entanglement with another parachutist.

I'm drifting nicely now, so I feel under my reserve for the two hooks that secure my backpack to my harness. It falls away to hang on a line 18 metres below. I'm supposed to work out the wind direction, but I'm out of time. In the final few seconds, the ground rushes up to meet me. As I hit, my forwards drift throws me on to my face, not quite the roll I expected. But as we say, a landing you get up from is a good landing.

CHAPTER 1 FLEEING LONDON, FEBRUARY 2002

London. A winter's day at the start of 2002. The South London pub's plate windows are steamed up, and cigarette smoke hangs in the air. It's full of Saturday-afternoon drinkers glad to escape the cold. Every time the door opens, patrons brace against the draught, and look up irritated, only relaxing when it swings shut. A big screen TV in the corner shows England about to kick off against Scotland, in the Rugby Six Nations.

We're at the bar. It's a chance to catch up with Dave and James as I'll be off to warmer climes in Australia, in little more than a week.

Dave is dark, lifts a bit of weights, and works offshore on oil rigs. He has just got back from the Congo, so is resting up. I've known him for a while, and we trained in the Army Reserve together. He's pleased to be a newly qualified pilot. James is an old flatmate—he's in local politics, which, as far as I can tell, is chairing interminable committees.

We sip our pints. I am keeping an eye on the game whilst James is engrossed in telling Dave a funny story from the previous week. There's some excitement, as on TV, Jason Robinson darts through to score for England.

"Is that Jeremy Guscott?" asks Dave, looking up amongst the cheering and noise.

"No–he's commentating mate," I reply. "Retired years ago."

I catch the barmaid's eye.

"My round, guys," I continue. She walks over. "Three pints of Stella Artois, please," I ask.

I look around and take in the London life all around me, knowing I'll be swapping it soon for the beaches and hotels of

Sydney. A middle-aged man wearing a nylon jacket and baseball cap interrupts my little reverie, pushing past me.

"S'cuse me please," he mutters.

I make way for him, edging closer to the bar, guarding my glass.

"Cheers mate. I'll see you in Australia, maybe, Steve. Let's fly together," Dave remarks.

"That would be great," I reply.

I can't go home, as my flat is currently being let out, so instead, I catch the bus back to my father's. As the bus winds its way through the London suburbs, across the grey Thames at Richmond bridge, I think back over the last few years.

Not even three years ago, my work for an American company had seen me seconded for two years on the continent in Luxembourg. It was a great place to live. I had an apartment, allowance and car. Long two-hour lunches, ski trips and European city destinations were the order of the day. That wasn't going to last forever, though, and eventually I returned to London and picked up life there. I bought a two-bed flat in South London and took on a new mortgage.

I was working for a financial institution on the 40th floor of Canary Wharf in Docklands. The view was spectacular, and we could gaze out and see tiny planes land and take off from City Airport. Ever since, though, it had seemed my life had been characterised by overtime, a glut of meetings, and cajoling managers. I could look forward to being mortgaged against the backdrop of London house price inflation and taking an uncertain place in the rat race. Then a year ago, a relationship with a girlfriend had ended.

As a young man, I had led a more adventurous, but meaningful life, toying with the military. I knew people talked about burning out and wondered if this was happening before my time. It did seem I needed a break.

I long had an ambition to visit Australia, and a year would do nicely. We had family in Sydney on the East coast. My father's Great Uncle filmed the First World War, in the trenches, and made a movie called *The Battle of the Somme*. It was seen by 20 million people all over the world—and descendants live in Melbourne. I was enthralled by the southern hemisphere rugby tradition, and wanted to see the faster pitches of my heroes down there, and Sydney was still basking in post-Olympic glory.

Fortuitously, I had learnt to ride at university, riding twice a week, helping out in the stables over the summer holidays, galloping across cold and blustering Exmoor, and riding out in Gloucestershire, so farming "jackeroo" work on stations was possible.

There was one snag. I had to apply for a visa before I turned 29. I was running out of time to raise the cash. Last spring, the issue was solved when my company announced they wanted me back in Luxembourg City, an opportunity to save. I counted the weeks of a continental summer and put cash away, but got down to the south of France for a break with a mate. We explored the Camargue region, and enjoyed *entrecote,* fries, and *salad nicoise.* Even the legions of mosquitoes could not defeat us.

Out of the blue, the events of 9/11 triggered a wave of layoffs as the turndown hit. There was uncertainty in the office as to who would stay and who would go. I approached the desk of my HR rep and volunteered myself for redundancy. Not only did I get my payout, but Australia House in the Strand issued a visa by return post, all in the nick of time.

So, as I walked back along the high street, I was days away from a new adventure. I hadn't been so excited in years.

***

Heathrow Airport. International Departures. On a Friday afternoon, I'm leaving for what I see as the last hurrah of my twenties—to join the trail of backpackers, mostly teenagers, to head "down under". I hoist my backpack onto the belt where it is whisked away. I've packed for a year away and have left a number for my tenants. The girl at security returns my passport.

"Thank you, Sir!" she says.

On the plane, I locate my row and fuss with the stowage of my pack in the overhead, allowing passengers to squeeze past. For this marathon Emirates flight over three legs, I have chosen the aisle seat so I can stretch out. It doesn't matter which way you go around the globe to Australia—it's a day either way. It's 17 hours *just* across the vast Pacific, if you choose to go via the US.

We land in Dubai and scoot through a connecting corridor to re-queue for the onward flight to Sydney. The desert sun spreads obliquely through the glass of the terminal, but the horizon is murky. There's a problem with my visa, and an official fixes it, fussing with the computer for worrying moments. Back on the plane, I track our progress across the Arabian Sea, then over India. With a case of the fidgets, I head to the rear near the galley where I find the crew and get a photo of them clowning around. There's a stop in Singapore, where we can stretch our legs. I stand at the gate under the gaze of a police Alsatian whilst passengers dash off to ritzy boutiques.

We make landfall on the Australian coastline near the Western Australian town of Broome. It would be easy to believe we are near Sydney, but of course, we still have to cross the desert interior. Make no mistake, it's a long way to Australia, and it's also a long way to traverse the largest island continent. It's a chance to nap, but an announcement from the captain wakes people from slumber.

"Ladies and Gentlemen, we will shortly be arriving in Sydney, good old Australia." He is a casual bloke with a nice line of folksy banter right out of the playbook, a sign of the relaxed world I hope to find. He concludes: "Wheels down soon."

The Antipodean sun slants through the windows as we descend over the New South Wales countryside, and I crane to see through the window at the dazzling harbour as we come into land. Once docked, waiting for the first-class passengers to disembark, I catch the eye of one of the cabin crew, and she smiles.

"How's it going?" she asks, beaming broadly.

"I'm fine, thanks," I reply. She seems a friendly sort.

"Have a great time in Australia," she says, as I file past.

The first person I come face-to-face on leaving the gate is another smiling girl in a patterned bikini—but she is a life-sized poster on the wall. Even in Australia, people don't wear beachwear at arrivals. There's a snaking queue for migration, and as the line moves, I shuffle forward a few paces waiting for a counter.

Katherine, my Australian friend, is meeting me. I know her from the London office a few years ago, and we've stayed in contact, messaging late in my day and early in hers. After several keen circuits of the arrivals hall, I find her.

"Katherine!" I call, and she turns around. "Wrong exit, eh?"

"Good to see you, Steve!" she smiles.

We embrace and eye each other up and down. She has short spiky, black hair; huge, dark green eyes and is wearing a pair of jeans, and a halter top. I suggest we get a car, and she nods in agreement. It's about 9:30 am by the time we get to the Hertz desk, but a chance to swap stories whilst the beleaguered attendant finds the keys.

I blink and squint in the morning sun. We thread our way through the rental lot, and are stopped by two men, driving to Melbourne, Australia's second city across the state border in Victoria, who need directions. Convinced they can make it by the afternoon, Katherine points out it will take them the best part of a day, maybe two.

"It's a long way boys," she calls after them.

I thought the men were Australian, but Katherine says they are Kiwis from "New Zulund".

"How can you tell the difference?" I ask her.

She explains the Kiwi accent is clipped, and has a lot less of a twang than the Australian dialect. Kiwis have a habit of swapping their vowels—Tasman Sea becomes "Tesmin Ci", and

"Cattle" becomes "Kettle". The most famous—ask any Australian —is "Fush und Chups" and "Tun Dollors and Sux Sints".

Katherine offers to drive and shows me the front page of the Sydney *Daily Telegraph*, with sombre news: the headlines in black reverse video report the death of Princess Margaret who passed away overnight.

First impressions: the suburbs of Sydney resemble the ones I saw in the US. It feels more like Los Angeles than London. There are no lines of drab terraced housing: detached Californian bungalows stand on blocks, surrounded by leafy trees and bushes. The light is particularly intense. This sun is a nice change after a gloomy UK winter, and it washes and presents houses and cafes in glorious stark technicolour. The Sunday traffic is light.

I suggest we head on down to Coogee, on the Eastern beaches, and find my accommodation, so take the beach road. Coogee is stunning, to be sure. The main entrance to the white sands is at a crossroads where Coogee Bay Road meets the road. The beach describes a concave arc, and we see an attractive paved plaza with locals roller-blading, walking or jogging. We look out to sea.

"So what do you think?" she says.

"It's just what I expected," I reply.

It *is* magnificent.

Looks like I am sorted. My accommodation is a few doors down. On one side: an array of breakfast cafes, and on the other side—the Coogee Bay Hotel. "Brekky" is at a corner café, with esplanade views. Katherine chooses the "Monster Breakfast" and I pick up the *Sydney Morning Herald* and make space when the coffee, toast, eggs, sausages and bacon arrive.

Katherine takes me to see her home in Lane Cove, a suburb on the north shore of the harbour. To get there, we need to take the Harbour Bridge, completed in 1932, and at the time of conception, the longest of its type in the world (although soon after opening, the Triboro Bridge in New York was found to be a bit longer.) As we approach, the huge hump—the "coat hanger" of the superstructure looms close. Katherine warns:

"Hold on. We're going over the hump," and giggles.

We pass through a masonry gateway, and the harbour folds out to our left and right. It is staggeringly beautiful. The water shimmers and glimmers in the morning sun. The Sydney Opera house is visible at the end of the peninsular extruding from Circular Quay, where ferries and fast catamarans arrive and depart. The Queen Elizabeth II is moored fast to the wharf, here on its annual visit to Sydney. To our left, a series of inlets and waterways heading inland. Opposite, the North Shore, Milson's Point and the business district of North Sydney. Further along: the exclusive suburb of Kirribili where the Prime Minister, John Howard, lives. The swish Upper-North Shore lies beyond.

Katherine lives in a quiet road sized wider than the average London street, in a timber, "weatherboard" house with a modest gum tree out front. I study this local example of fauna and marvel at its colour and texture.

"Come *on!*" Katherine says.

We go in and have a look round. I notice an air-conditioning unit on the wall; as Australian homes are otherwise in the main unheated, it also serves as a heater in the winter. There is an outside dunny (loo) which she points out proudly. It's in a wooden shed. Out of curiosity, I stick my head around the door. According to lore, I don't suppose there are any redback spiders to trap the unwary? She rolls her eyes.

On the way back to town, I see a sign for an AFL—Australian Football League game. Seeing an "Aussie Rules Game" is high on my list of things to do, so I implore Katherine to go. She agrees, and we drive to the North Sydney Oval, and soon we are enjoying a steak sandwich outside the stands. I can see that old stalwart Tony "Plugger" Lockett is making his comeback today in this pre-season game: Sydney Swans are playing Essendon, a Victorian team from Melbourne.

Australian Rules football was first codified in the 19th century. A story goes it was a means for cricketers to keep fit in the off-season. It was formerly a Melbourne-based Victorian Football League, but now teams from all over Australia play in a single league. Brisbane in Queensland fields the Lions, a team that currently holds the Championship, (much to the disgust of Victorian fans.)

Aussie Rules is not huge, here—Sydneysiders refer to it as "Aerial Ping Pong". Here on the East coast, rugby is the preferred game with 13-a side Rugby League played in the National Rugby League (NRL). My game, Rugby Union (15 players) is also played, but is considered rather elitist and is denigrated as being for private school "*rah rahs*." Katherine explained "Rugby's *rah-rah*!"

Before kick-off, Katherine and I stroll around the kiosks looking at the t-shirts, *eskies* (coolers) and souvenirs. I spot a line of neoprene cups emblazoned with the Essendon insignia.

"What's this, mate?" I ask the stallholder.

"It's a *stubby* holder," chimes Katherine. "It keeps your beer cold."

"Useful," I reply.

Katherine threads through the afternoon crowd and I study the game. The game is athletic and free-flowing—the main skill involves running and jumping to catch a cross-field kick. When a player catches a ball, he gets a free kick. A player can also "handball" to a teammate or can bounce it on the ground every few steps on the run. It looks frenetic.

We are surrounded by rather sunburnt, dishevelled fans. An older man with leathery skin leans forward and cups his hands to his mouth:

"WHAT–DO–WE–THINK–OF–PLUGGER?!"

The response from the crowd:

"HE'S –ALLLLRIIIIIGHHHHT!"

"HOW–DOES–HE–DO-IT!?"—the older man again. Crowd:

"E–A–S–Y!!"

Everyone grins. Every time a player scores between the posts for a full six points, the goal umpire points with both index fingers, shoulder-width apart.

"How big is it?!" shouts the crowd.

If the player scores a "behind", outside the main posts, the umpire indicates with just the one arm. ("How small is it?!" they shout.)

Freshening up, we head to the Coogee Bay Hotel for a pub meal, surrounded by a melee of locals and backpackers: boys in surf t-shirts and girls in sarongs who are enjoying the balmy evening. It occurs to me that back in London, people are shivering through their winter morning. I'm struggling, though, to keep my eyes open as my body clock is on London time.

"Let's head back," says Katherine. "You're fading, Steve."

***

I awake to my first Australian summer dawn. There is a bird outside calling with a crazy, laughter-like sound. This turns out to be a Kookaburra, an outsized bird with a large head and beak which looks like a Kingfisher.

I'll drop off Katherine on the North Shore, and she gives me directions towards the Harbour bridge.

"This is where you need to turn, Steve," she indicates.

Approaching the turnoff, I fail to make it, and end up driving through the Harbour tunnel. What's more, I discover I have no money for the toll and receive a ticket. Desite these nuisances I get her to work, and the car back to the rental. Time to scout out the city.

I head into the Central Business District and look around. First impressions: despite the rush hour, what strikes me is that there are less people around like you'd see in a European capital like London or Paris. There is no need to thread my way or avoid loud throngs of tourists. Relaxed men and women in business dress stroll casually down the road. The train I have just got off is busy, but not crammed wall-to-wall like the London Underground. People sit calm and collected and may even smile at you. And pedestrian crossings: the loud, intermittent, cross signal sounds like a chicken clucking—another difference—and facet of Australian city life.

Katherine is going to meet me after work in a bar not far from Town Hall in the Central Business District. I'm walking north towards Circular Quay along George Street, one of the main thoroughfares.

Opposite Town Hall, I find a bar called Hotel Coronation and get the last two stools at the counter. The bar is full of office workers enjoying an after-work beer, and I order a schooner of Hahn whilst I wait. Katherine waltzes in; she flops down, and I get her a drink. Thus refreshed, we head down Pitt Street Mall, up towards Circular Quay in search of a meal. We turn past the ferry wharves taking people across the Harbour to places like Manly on the Northern Beaches and salubrious destinations on the southern side.

The Opera House is dead ahead. The "coat hanger" looms above us to our left. The Queen Elizabeth II liner is still at her moorings. To our right, an art-house cinema—and restaurants have placed tables out for evening diners. We choose Thai and a spot overlooking the liner, and the lights of the Harbour. The Chicken Szechuan looks good. As we are tucking in, the liner gets underway, pulling serenely away from her berth and from somewhere, a brass band strikes up to distant applause. The location: prime Sydney. After a few beers, I am feeling warm, good-natured and happy to be "away" as we walk back along the Quay. There could be endless possibilities this year.

"Enjoying Sydney, Steve?" she says.

"It's great, Katherine," I reply.

***

I am in my room when there is an announcement on the PA that anyone wanting work must get to the phone. I amble out and get talking to Jeremy. He's a tree surgeon and asks me if I want work. I accept; he'll pick me up at 7am tomorrow morning.

I stand on the steps and wait, eating an impromptu breakfast of milk and fruit, wearing old shorts and a faded South African rugby top. Jeremy is prompt, and arrives in a pickup, and with Shakira singing "Everywhere" on the radio talk back station, drives me to where the rest of the gang have assembled. He points out his offsider, a wiry, sinewy Kiwi—and a backup guy, who drives a van trailing a wood chipper.

The business of pruning trees turns out to grant access to beautiful, affluent suburbs and prestige properties with laid-out manicured gardens ("yards"). We pull up in a side street close to the CBD, and walk down a long flight of steps. We find ourselves on a lawn next to water under a canopy of trees. Peering around, I find myself standing on the very edge of Sydney Harbour. The Harbour Bridge spans my entire field of vision. Across the water, nestling alongside Milson's Point is the facade of Luna amusement park. The Opera House is still resplendent in the sun.

But we must get to work: Jeremy pulls on his safety helmet, and steps into his climbing harness. He's got a pair of spikes, which he is wearing like cavalry spurs. With these and a sling, he can climb pretty much any tree he fancies. He reaches around for the chainsaw he has slung over his back and shouts a warning as branches fall for collection. We haul them away to be mulched.

I spend the next two hours carrying logs up the flight of stairs loaded and skipping back down unencumbered. It is very hot, and soon my shoulders and brow are soaked with sweat, so I take off my shirt, which has afforded my shoulders protection from splinters. I put it back on 15 minutes later, when I realise my exposed shoulders have a slight glow from the sun.

Jeremy calls a break for lunch, and we perch on newly-split aromatic eucalypt logs admiring the view, tucking into sandwiches. Should I be paying Jeremy, I ask? He pays me there and then, handing me notes from a fistful, one a time. I have no idea what the rate is, so when I look hesitant, he slips me one more plastic fifty dollar note, hardly breaking rhythm.

We crane around when we hear giggling. Next door, there's a swimming pool, set in the lawn of a Federation (early 1900s) mansion with a period filigree wrought-iron facade. A bevy of girls lounging on recliners pose for a squad of photographers, all jostling for shots.

Welcome to the Emerald City high life.

CHAPTER 2 BACKPACKER LIFE

I am woken early by the laughter of kookaburras and the calls of other assorted native Antipodean wildlife, but soon drift off again, wrapped in a silk sleeping bag liner with my legs sticking out at the end. The hostel tannoy stirs me again at 8am.

"Checkout time is 9.30. If you haven't paid for tonight, your fee is due. Checkout time is..." [This is the English girl on reception].

"Shut up..." murmurs one of the blokes across from me.

I lie still, luxuriating in the knowledge that there are no deadlines due, or meetings scheduled, as would normally be the case in my day.

Satisfied, I open my eyes and look around the dorm, a six-bed basement room opposite from the communal showers and toilets. I've got the bottom bunk: this is the choice location—you can sit amidst your gear and get organised, and getting into bed, inebriated or not, is easier. The novices, of course, head for the top bunks like on school trips.

Backpacker dorms on Sydney's Eastern Beaches are not exactly spick and span. The floors are covered in dirty clothes, half-read novels, travel guides (the *Rough Guide* or *Lonely Planet*), shoe boxes and clothes shop bags. Backpackers suss the dress standard and then dash off to buy beachwear, supporting the local boutiques. Once a week, a cleaner arrives, and sweeps the detritus into a corner for collection. Every power point has a mobile phone or camera on charge. Most of my fellow tourists are teenagers travelling before or after degree courses: I'm a bit of an old-sweat, in fact.

I pull on a singlet, *thongs* (flip flops), and head to the beach, threading my way through the sunbathers—weekends see it fill up—till I find a choice spot. The safest parts of the beach are marked by two red and yellow flags. The advice is: "Swim between the Flags". The lifeguards wear distinctive yellow and red swim-hats, and loose-fitting protective shirts.

It's 30 degrees, but it hardly registers now. I am acclimatising, and the heat in Australia is a rather dry sort: more favourable, perhaps, than the sticky heat waves of the UK. In London, 27 degrees is fan-fared in the papers with photos of people seeking relief in Hyde Park fountains. A day less than 23 degrees is cool in the height of a Sydney summer.

After half an hour, something else registers: that sun has a bite: the *Daily Telegraph* forecasts the UV index over 13—that's blisteringly high. Australian friends have warned me that skin can burn in minutes.

"The sun is *different* here," Katherine said.

An expat friend who is off working on oil rigs tells me to stay out of the sun when it shows white and wait until it turns red in the late afternoon. On TV, there's a famous, long-running, public information commercial called "Slip Slap Slop", as in "Slip on a T-Shirt, Slap on a hat, and Slop on some suncream", now in its 20th year. One last thing: the locals don't sunbathe—that wouldn't cut the mustard—they sunbake. Sun-tan lotion is by necessity, sunblock.

I plan to visit the zoo on the north shore of the harbour. If I am to get farm work, I need to kit myself out with gear to wear "upcountry" so will stop off in the CBD on the way in.

The bus stop is right by the beach with commanding views of the sea and the heads. There's still lots of people running, walking, standing around enjoying summer. We meander to Bondi Junction, a hub for people heading to town. Hotels (pubs) and buildings have a characteristic metal awning over the ground floor like a brimmed hat. I mooch around the shops and browse the second-hand book stores. I'm in luck—I find a book called *The Cowboy Way,* by an American author, which is about the year he spent on a cattle station in "big sky" Montana; with insights for the taking—and an erudite, dusty hardback

Handbook for Jackeroos. And an autobiography of Australia's talented cricketer Shane Warne.

On Market Street, in the CBD, I locate Sydney's well-known outfitter emporium Gowings, which combines a camping shop with a clothing store. I buy a waxed Driz-a-Bone waterproof (for the "wet") and a broad-brimmed felt Akubra hat called a "Cattleman" (for the "dry".) The Akubra brand is uniquely Australian, a supplier to country people for generations. There aren't any corks on this hat though.

At Circular Quay, a map tells me I can get to Taronga zoo by boarding a ferry leaving from Wharf Two. I stand with tourists and workers who have congregated at the bow to admire the view. Imagine being a commuter—one of the great attractions of Sydney life is plying the harbour on a working day. The towers of the CBD stretch into the sky behind us and the handsome residences of the north side of the harbour flit past. The ferry leaves us at the wharf. We have the option of catching a bus to the zoo entrance or swing in an intrepid gondola car to the top of the cliff. The gondola option takes minutes to the gate, where I am relieved of 12 dollars.

I head for my old childhood favourites, the lions and tigers. But I can't, in all conscience, miss the Antipodean wildlife—Kangaroos, Wombats and Koalas. I discover the red kangaroo is Australia's largest kangaroo, weighing up to 90 kilogrammes, and standing almost two metres tall. I pay a pilgrimage to the house containing the spiders, to see the Redback and the lethal Sydney Funnel Web which rises up on its back legs when it feels threatened. (I have no idea how it knows to stay in Sydney.)

Part of the zoo runs along the cliff-top, and I find a small seating area in a natural amphitheatre. It is possible to see across the harbour to Rushcutter's Bay and the south shore, resplendent on a picture-postcard day like this. Yachts are at anchor, and I see the speck of a canoeist bobbing on the water. Predictably, the exit for the zoo channels me through the shop, and I notice I have caught the sun from my stroll: my face is pink in the lights.

In many cities I have visited, it's good to go high and get your bearings: there is still time to get to the AMP Tower, a tower in the centre of the CBD, halfway down Elizabeth. At the top near the observation deck, the owners offer the "Skydome" experience, which includes interactive displays and a virtual reality roller coaster ride.

The display starts with a slideshow, where a holographic Australian man and woman are projected, depicted in various scenarios in town and country. We see him standing next to a ute, on a property in South Australia at dusk, watching Emus race past, before finding him in a flat on the rooftops of a city talking to her. The man is portrayed as the typical Aussie male living in the outback or country town; laid-back, obsessed with "footy", whereas the woman is the archetypal "Sheila".

In a modest viewing theatre, we strap into roller coaster-like seats and the lights dim, and soon, with accompanying jerks from the seats, we are racing in a tiny helicopter in a cattle muster in the Kimberleys, or canoeing rapids in the Northern Territory. We even find ourselves on the pitch of the Melbourne Cricket Ground in the middle of an AFL game, before whizzing along Katherine Gorge. The exit leads out on to the observation deck. I can see the Eastern beaches and the North Shore gleaming in the sunshine.

I stroll to Woolworths to pick up dinner. First surprise—Rick Astley is singing "Never Gonna Give You Up" from around 1987. I am transported back to my childhood. For young players: under New South Wales licencing laws, alcohol is not sold in supermarkets, so there is an opportunity to skip through a open door into an adjoining bottle shop should the need arise. A teenaged girl at the checkout smiles at me.

"How you ga-in?" she asks, in a sing-song voice.

"I'm good, thanks," I reply.

Australians seem to say this with a capital G. They don't say "Fine, thank you." She grins cheekily:

"So, how's your day been?"

"OK. And yours?" I inquire.

It would be rude not to.

"*Good*," she says.

Is everyone so damn happy? (I put it down to the weather.)

Back in the hostel kitchen, I ponder my shopping. The fresh goods go into the huge communal refrigerator—name and room number. (Evidently, some like the challenge of hunting their food by shape and smell.) Backpackers drift in from the beach and jobs. I happily simmer my spaghetti bolognaise, passing the time of day with people. A Dutch girl stops and says it smells good. She waves a spoon. Can she try some?

"That is very good," she says.

An Irish girl comes by and starts a conversation.

"You were here yesterday, weren't you?"

"Yup, I'm Steve," I reply.

She's from Dublin. She offers me chocolate biscuits: Tim-Tams, Australia's answer to chocolate Penguins, and shows me her blog. An outside staircase leads to the ground-floor patio and a yard with a clothes line. Backpackers sit on chairs smoking. One enterprising bloke with a guitar has an easy mechanism with which to approach girls.

"Hello–will you be my girlfriend?"

It doesn't look like he has much success so far.

It's still warm, and the sun is definitely over the yardarm. Time for a "cold one"—no excuse for warm London beer here, and even travellers have pre-dinner drinks. The Irish girl accompanies me to the bottle shop (off-licence) a few doors up the beach road. The fun part is walking into chilled rooms, a respite from the heat outside. We can buy beer in "slabs" (crates) or "cartons" (boxes). A slab holds "tinnies" (cans); cartons hold "stubbies" (bottles.) By the looks of it, most backpackers get by on cheap four litre casks of wine—it saves them from getting to grips with a whole new Antipodean language.

Time to head over to the Coogee Bay Hotel with people. There's the Irish girl and Dutch girl; a short, stocky bloke from Hastings, and his mate, a 6ft 4in strapping body builder. In the outside beer garden, I order a round of drinks, getting a schooner of Hahn for myself.

What's a schooner? Drinks measures in Australia are confusing, depending on what State you've ordered in. In New South Wales, a regular beer is a schooner, which is 425 ml, about three-quarters of a British pint. A midi is half a pint. That pint you'd order in a London boozer, or in a Munich beer tent would be warm by the time you got to the bottom, which would try the most patient of people. In Adelaide, South Australia, though, a schooner is a *pint*. A Darwin stubbie, in the Northern Territory, on the other hand, is *several* pints—for when you're thirsty.

Feeling cheerful, I slip back out, and meet up with Katherine and her friends in a pub hosting a live band in North Sydney. In the small hours, we head to Darling Harbour, a dazzling array of bars, attractions, cinemas and ice cream parlours packed with revellers, near Circular Quay, and find a sports bar showing the Ireland-England game from London, with scores of English and Irish alike, watching the action on a big TV.

***

Last year, in London, Dave and his housemate had regaled me with their flying stories. Dave had moved to a new house on the Thames at Rotherhithe, so when I finished work at Canary Wharf, we would meet for a beer in the Slug and Lettuce. The housemate was taking flying lessons, and was excited about it, so it wasn't long before Dave took it up. When he wasn't on shift on the Jubilee Line Extension, Dave was therefore driving up to Norfolk to fly at a RAF base.

It seems to me that whilst I'm in Australia there's no point in sitting on a beach every day watching my dollars earn interest: I need to keep challenged in my year off, so I figure that still fresh from hearing about Dave's flying, I may as well give it a shot myself.

Bankstown airport is in Sydney's outer south-west away from the shore. The south-west does not quite have the cachet of the beachside suburbs. It is home to a sizeable Lebanese population amongst others. It has a different reputation—hotspots make their way on to the news for the occasional stabbing or gang-related crime. In some ways, the outer Western Suburbs are the poorer cousins—there is a bit of a stigma attached to being a "Westie".

What's more, there's a flying school at the airport.

CHAPTER 3 LOOPING THE LOOP
– THE BEAUTIFUL PEOPLE

A typical flying day sees me making my way over to the school office, where I sign for the plane and collect the paperwork and keys. A back door faces a gate in a fence, which provides access to the flight-line and to a grass area where the school keep their aeroplanes parked in neat, orderly lines. Even at 9am, it's warm, and the heat rises from the tarmac, and the runways shimmer in the haze.

I circle the aircraft. I check that the ailerons, elevators and rudder are working and clamber on to the wings to check the fuel. My instructor, Wes, arrives and takes the right-hand seat of the cockpit as "Pilot-In-Command". He wears a crisp white shirt with black epaulettes. He's only 21. Despite his youth, he is a grade three instructor, and holds a Commercial Pilot's Licence, and has 600 hours of logged flying time. This accrued experience counts towards the number of hours he needs for his dream job with an airline like Qantas, so really, he's just working his ticket.

"Beautiful morning," he says.

"Good one, for it, eh?" I reply.

In the left-hand seat, the pilot's seat, I've go through the pre-flight checklist. Satisfied, I nod at Wes and lean out of the window and shout:

"Clear Prop!" turn the ignition key, and the propellor spins into life.

"Let's go, Steve," Wes says.

We crawl down the apron to the run-up bays as if we were in a supermarket carpark. I check the engine, taking the revs up, holding the aircraft with the brakes.

Then I taxi nervously to the holding point, indicated by a

wooden sign on the grass. Reading the runway number, I depress the mike key and announce:

"Bankstown tower, this is Cessna Sierra–Lima–Bravo: Ready: runway–er–one-two-seven left, ready for upwind departure."

They respond:

"Cessna SLB hold for inbound traffic."

We'd ordinarily be granted permission to line up on the runway, but "control" is expecting a large jet aircraft in, and we need to wait. They don't forget us and get back:

"Sierra–Lima–Bravo: cleared for takeoff Runway 127 left." I parrot back:

"Cleared for takeoff, Sierra–Lima–Bravo."

Best to make sure. My mouth is all of a sudden dry.

Looking both ways, like joining a main road, I line up at the start of the runway. I engage throttle smoothly and soon we are trundling along, gathering speed. I keep us awkwardly in the middle with small foot adjustments on the rudder, and pull back at 65 knots, about the speed you'd drive along a highway. The Cessna climbs gingerly at a shallow angle, wallowing as she does. That's all well and good, but the houses and fields track below making me feel giddy.

"That's looking good, Steve," Wes says.

Once we get up there, we are buffeted by wind, which made me feel nervous and uneasy at first. It's a beautiful day, though, and my nerves soon fade.

At several thousand feet, over the suburbs, I can see Sydney laid out below. It has an immense suburban sprawl: considerably larger than London. I can see Richmond and Windsor—comprising houses, backyards, and the occasional shimmering swimming pool. There are housing estates with pristine two-story "McMansions", houses with multiple bedrooms and a theatre room with tiny concrete yards, with a pergola, in sheet steel or "colorbond" (any colour you like). The light reflects off these whilst I practise climbs and descents for 30 minutes—sort of a slow yo-yo through the ether. Then turns—for the first goes, I lose my starting point on the horizon and after unwinding the roll I discover I was not quite heading where I thought I would be. Wes leans over occasionally to tweak a setting or mutter a word of appraisal.

Back at the runway, the wind is rustling across the runway, sending the flags horizontal, so Wes takes over and shows me how to crab the plane in, holding it to one side as we descend. He makes the landing look easy.

The flying lessons are interspersed with ground school; briefs given to me in the portacabins by the young master. He sits across a table from me sipping from a carton of double-shot iced-coffee, and we go through a side of A4. On the syllabus: subjects like "Emergency Landings"; "Level flight, Ascending and Descending." In the hostel, I study my *Basic Aeronautical Knowledge book,* and *Flight Radio for Pilots.* There's a fair bit of homework.

Seeking a break from hostel kitchen food, we have been exploring the restaurants on Coogee Bay road. A group of us try seafood in a boutique diner, tucking into Paella enjoying the aromas of saffron and chicken, washed down with craft beer, then head out to see England play in the rugby (or "rah-rah" as the locals call it.) In the Coogee Bay Hotel, I bump into a young crowd from the hostel. The team comes unstuck at the final hurdle against France, so yet another Grand Slam goes beckoning. A whole crowd of raucous English expats crowded into the bar are crestfallen. In the street, with pizza delivery drivers having a smoke, I chat to teenage girls who ask me how old I am. One takes a drag from a cigarette and says:

"I've seen you around. You're dead handsome–for an old fella," she corrects herself.

I'm not sure if that is a compliment—but I will take it.

***

The sun at noon is already hanging lower in the sky, and the first week of March, the southern autumn, the renowned Mardi Gras weekend arrives, and many backpackers will be off to watch the floats and procession, but I've been invited to a bar-b-que in Cremourne on the North Shore.

I was running my customary route along the beach path, when I heard my name called out, so I pulled up, and looked back. I recognised a bloke waving at me. It was Mike, a West Australian from Perth, who used to sit opposite me at work in the tower at Canary Wharf. He was last seen leaving for South America, and is catching up with family in Sydney, and it's sheer chance we have bumped in to each other.

"Mate! What are the chances?" he cries. "Come over tonight. My brother Isaac, will pick you up, 6pm," he tells me.

I pop into the bottle shop on Coogee Bay Road and buy a slab of James Boaig. Isaac pulls up in a 4x4, with the legend of a plumbing service emblazoned on the side, and the back-tray cage fitted with a green tarp. Inside the cab, I am greeted by a friendly Staffordshire bull terrier.

Isaac and a mate are travelling around Australia in this vehicle —equipped to cross deserts and sleeping under the stars in swags. Isaac has jet-black, neatly razored hair and a physique honed by surfing. He grabs one of my stubbies, and taking a stubby holder looped on the gear stick, cracks it open, and sets off towards the Harbour bridge.

"Good beer, mate," he says.

Mike greets me at the apartment. He is handling tongs, presiding over the bar-b-que, and serves up prawns and pork cutlets which we devour before we sit outside and chat about life in London. Isaac shows video of them crossing the Nullarbor desert in Western Australia and visiting a barren property that he lived on as a boy, with the sound of a wind coming in off the desert on the audio.

In the morning, we take photos of us standing by the 4x4, with Isaac propped on the bonnet—we pile in, and they drop me off at Milson's Point, and I walk across the Harbour Bridge.

Halfway, I stop and admire the sweeping vista, one of the world's truly great locations. I can spot the waterfront property I worked on in my first week. The roads back are littered with tins and takeaway polystyrene from the fallout from the night's partying.

I have now graduated to flying circuits around Bankstown, where taking off, flying, and landing are practised over and over again. It can be infuriatingly frustrating; one circuit is nigh on perfect, the next a dog's dinner. One morning, the forecast is not favourable—not such good weather for circuits, but, we can still fly, so we decide to go for a joy-flight to Sydney and back.

Wes directs me towards the harbour bridge from the north-west. This is the only direction, as the south is too close to flight paths. As we draw near to the harbour, it starts to spit, so I focus on the flying and less of the looking. The rain clears, and we cruise over the northern suburbs to Hornsby, which is recognisable by the "sheds" at the train depot. My aunt and uncle live down there somewhere.

"Hello Bankstown Tower, this is Cessna Sierra–Lima– Bravo, downwind for final stop. Request Northern Side," I say into my headset.I give my door a nudge and Wes tugs his seat belt—all OK. Everything checks out.

"Cessna Sierra–Lima–Bravo: cleared for full stop," replies the tower duty operator.

Surely a perfect radio call? but my focus is soon broken:

"Come on, Steve. What are you going to do?"

Wes is nagging me as I have failed to maintain height.

I'm so busy flying the downwind leg, parallel to the runway, I have forgotten to trim the plane. We have lost 200 feet already.

I extend the flaps, and roll on to the base leg, side-on to the runway. I'm straining to see over Wes, and after we cross a lake, I sight the runway coming up on our right-hand side: he leans back so I can see. I turn again to line up, and unwind the languid roll as it slides under our nose.

I swallow hard. I slow to 65 knots, watching the rate of

descent. I apply more power as at this rate, I'm going to hit the road in front of the runway. Wes grunts his approval.

65 knots. (Check airspeed—*again.*)

"Cessna SLB–Clear for landing," interrupts the tower. I repeat that back. We're not just playing games on the radio here—days later, there was a collision resulting in a fatal crash.

As we are guaranteed to make the runway, I cut power and allow the aeroplane to float over the threshold. I pull back—*gently*—and now we are six feet off the tarmac sinking. The idea is to "hold off" to scrub the speed before touchdown. It's not too bad, and whilst the landing is not exactly a "greaser", we get down. I hit the brakes and angle the nose straight for the taxiway.

As seen from the sky, my paternal aunt and uncle live in Hornsby Heights, a leafy suburb on the edge of the northern suburbs, close to a National park, and I get the train up for an afternoon tea. There are several minutes of confusion when I exit the station on the wrong side of the tracks, but soon I find my aunt waving at me, and we are reunited with my uncle at the car.

They take me back to their comfortable 4-bedroom villa: and I get a preview of how they have been spending their retirement. Many homes are erected with a timber pine frame and cladded with brick—universally known as "brick veneer". I am impressed with the large sundeck and pool. The deck is elevated, and the bar-b-que is the size of an Aga back home in England. She takes me around the garden with the camellias and frangipani and when we get to the smart landscaped swimming pool, asks me not to mention it to my uncle.

"He'll only talk about the expense of it all," she says.

So much for the glee of retirement.

Back at the hostel, I've noticed on my strolls around Coogee the way the beach is swarming with "the beautiful people". And it's not just the drinkers, revellers or diners, it's the fitness fanatics. Living here is like being in California, 90210. In the parks and across the cliffs on the beach heads, I sight a constant stream of joggers and runners. Blokes in Speedos run up the beach, alternately sprinting and recovering. You wouldn't wear Speedos at the beach in England—but it's quite normal here. The streets are full of long-haired blokes in wet suits. The Dutch and Germans vie to get in the water. Boys and girls walk along the street dripping with water, with newly acquired boards slung under one arm.

Australia's alfresco outdoors lifestyle, and the endless opportunity for sport and leisure is not completely lost on me. Every day, I am running along Coogee Beach, occasionally running barefoot along the water's edge, or skimming through the surf. If I am feeling energetic, I run the Eastern Suburb's beach walk: eight kilometres, which runs from Coogee to Bondi.

("Bond-I, Steve, not Bond-ee," said Katherine.)

Today, I'll run it there and back. I set off down Coogee Bay Road, side-stepping the tourists, locals and backpackers. At the lights, I wait for the green man, and run on to the plaza past the showers where a girl in a bikini is finishing rinsing. She briefly slips her hand too far down her bottoms, and I get a glimpse of a round, sumptuous buttock. The plaza continues to the road, which peters out at the end of the beach at a restaurant, and a path snakes up a grassy hill. I run to the top, which is the headland for the north side of Coogee beach.

The path progresses along the flat before descending towards a cove. This has steps cut out into it, requiring care. The route is shaded by overhanging trees and bushes, and walkers with dogs see brightly coloured yellow Orc Spiders nestling in webs. The sea comes back into view. Then a climb up wooden flights of stairs back up to the top. It's all good exercise for the calf muscles.

This is Gordon's Point: an area used by scuba diving schools —then to Clovelly, which is on the other side of the head. Here, there is a beach inlet. Water has been channelled off into a sea swimming pool on the edge and swimmers complete lengths, and mothers with children splash around in the shallows.

Up a sharp hill, skirting a restaurant there, I'm starting to feel the pace. On to grass and past a cemetery. The path negotiates the edge of this, with a sharp drop to the Pacific Ocean on the other side. Walkers squeeze by in single file.

I descend to Bronte Beach. It's smaller than Coogee, appointed with a children's train ride circling in the trees, with glamorous "Yummy Mummies" cooing over pre-schoolers. Past the Surf Lifesaver's club. I detour away from the beach to the main road, stopping long enough to buy a bottle of Gatorade.

I tighten my shoulder straps, and hydrated, climb the steps outside the lifesaver's club there and head toward Tamarama beach on the final leg to Bondi. The road curves at a café, and finally, at another headland, the mile-long stretch of Bondi Beach looms in to view; it's a bigger, and louder version of Coogee. It's the most famous beach in Australia.

CHAPTER 4 "INTRODUCTION TO AGRICULTURE"

Prior to my arrival in Australia, I was inspired by the nation's colonial heritage and roots. Like most Englishmen, a lot of my knowledge of Australia started from photos I had seen at school of the outback and cattle stations ("properties" not farms, "homesteads", not farmhouses: the names seem to paint a rather different picture of rural life.) I uncovered colour spreads of the "Flying Doctors", and the "School of the Air" in annuals and the Sunday Supplements.

The record shows the difficulties experienced by the original settlers working on the land in trying conditions, yet persevering and turning the country from an agricultural settlement to an industrialised country in 200 years. The farming husbandry of the vast, inhospitable countryside is a continuous trait in Australian history.

From a comfortable sofa in the hostel, I have seen "outback adventure" shows on tv. One is called *Troy Dann's Outback Adventures*, and the bushman seems to spend his daylight hours alternately in his ute—"utility" (pickup), on motorbike, or flying over the Kimberley in his helicopter, wrestling with cattle, or barrelling in the dust on his bike. If truth be told, I am quite tickled by this boy's own existence. As a keen rider, and no stranger to adversity, I can identify with the hardships of the outdoor stockman. In fact, I'd like to give it a go myself. Nothing ventured, nothing gained.

So, I've got myself on to a course run on a property in sub-tropical Queensland over the northern border. It's imaginatively called "Introduction to Agriculture" and aims to teach novice Jackeroos and Jillaroos—station hands or roustabouts—skills that will make them employable in the eyes of future employers.

This is run by a retired English couple who will hand us out to farming families game enough to teach us. We will be introduced to working on motorbikes and horseback, with sheep and cattle; to drive a tractor, repair fences and irrigate fields. A job somewhere in Australia then awaits.

***

A minibus sets me down at the domestic terminal at Kingsford-Smith. A Virgin Blue flight traverses New South Wales and hops across the border into Queensland, flying over the glamorous Gold Coast to sub-tropical Brisbane. The plane is crewed by a most friendly and quick-witted cabin crew, and they keep us entertained in-flight, with wisecracks and jokes. One is a recent reference to a competitor—Ansett's demise in 2001.

On arrival, I wind my watch back an hour as Queensland does not observe daylight savings time. [Ask someone from New South Wales why this is so, and they will tell you it is because the "Banana Benders", as Queenslanders are referred to, complained the extra light bleached the curtains.]

"It's different up there," remarked Katherine's father. "Life is a bit slower than in Sydney–you could be in a queue in a paper shop, and in a rush for the weekly coach service to the next town and the attitude will be 'She'll be alright'–it'll be there next week."

It's also more humid here, given the latitude, and I wipe my brow a bit more than down south, rushing for the monorail which connects the airport with the Roma Street bus terminal. I am just in time for the next bus.

Travelling on the Greyhound bus through the outskirts of Brisbane, I see examples of the archetypal Queenslander; wood-clad houses elevated on stilts designed such that any breeze blows under them and cools them down in the hot, sticky summers.

The bus winds its way through the Sunshine Coast towns of Caloundra, Mooloolaba, and Noosa, and thence inland to the mining town of Gympie. The coast affords the people that live there beach life, sport, year-round warmth and short, sunny winters, and there's also hinter land and national parks to explore. Many people retire to this region from colder, Melbourne and Sydney down south, where the winters are perhaps more insufferable. The bus makes a stop at a rest stop on the main highway, at a "servo" (Service station).

At Gympie, I find I am not far from the Sunshine Coast, near the tourist attractions of Rainbow Beach and Fraser Island. The bus service through to Goomeri, my final destination, leaves once a week, and I have planned my timetable accordingly, so it leaves not long after I get in. I settle into my seat for the last leg of the journey, and as we leave Gympie bus station, I spot to my chagrin my travel towel still draped over the railings outside —still, I cheer myself up by studying the bus driver, an older gent who taps his fingers on the wheel to country music piped through the PA system.

When we arrive in Goomeri, a young bloke, James, has turned up from the farm to meet and greet. We disembark, and James takes names and supervises course attendees chucking their gear on the back of his ute, a twin-cab Holden Jackeroo. However, as we discover, me and an English girl called Sally must stay behind as the course starts tomorrow, Tuesday, and pickups today only apply to those who pre-booked from England.

Therefore, we'll spend the night in the local hotel in a town which looks like it's straight out of a cowboy western. It is deathly quiet, a collection of streets with a newspaper agency, a general store called the Goomeri Emporium and the hotel plus a big supermarket. A large outdoor swimming pool is deserted.

Rooms are cheap at the hotel—only 18 bucks a night, but they don't accept EFTPOS as the line is down. The nearest ATM is 25 miles down the road, and Sally needs cash, so the manager offers to take Sally there.

I tag along, as I fancy seeing more of the Queensland countryside. We're there in no time at all, driving through the lush scenery which has red, golden, and green hues. The green is a lime shade—different to the dark green of European fields. (Ask the Australian Impressionists.) I'm left parked behind an old Holden Ute which is essentially a car with a tray on the back. A dog chained in the backs looks at me quizzically.

Sally returns and holds out her hand for a lick when they get back.

"Oh–Steve! He's gorgeous. Is he a Blue Heeler?" she asks the manager.

"Yes, he would be, that's right," she says, pointing her fob at her car to unlock it.

The manager explains that under recent Australian legislation, all dogs must be restrained so they can't leap over the side. The Blue Heeler is a quintessential breed.

Back at the hotel, we relax at the bar and order drinks. I order a Victoria Bitter or VB (without a doubt the most prolific beer, available country-wide), Sally goes for a Cider. (Castlemaine XXXX is the brand of choice around here in the "Banana Bender" State.) The barmaid hands over the change:

"There you go, Darl."

"Darl" is pronounced "Doll": and appears to be an affectionate term used. I look around at the bar. There are a few regulars sitting around eyeing me and Sally. They look like they could be extras in *Crocodile Dundee*. The men are grizzled, and have line-ridden, pock-marked faces by a lifetime of sun exposure. They wear flannel shirts, jeans, and paddock boots of all sorts and makes. I am wearing pretty much the same, a pair of chinos, paddock boots, and an old tatty Calvin Klein shirt.

Sally and I pass the time chatting about our lives in the UK and in Australia. She tells me about her recent WOOFing experiences in New Zealand. She's a rider and is hoping to get a job with horses.

As we're getting peckish, I order a t-bone and chips, and Sally, a vegetarian, orders Thai. We are re-seated in the run-down dining room next door to the saloon with a grandiose sweeping staircase to the rooms above. A poster somewhat vicariously recounts the glories of the Brisbane Broncos football team. The barmaid brings my steak. It takes up the entire plate, liberally drenched in pepper sauce, and the chips and salad vie for attention on an "overflow" plate. It looks like something out of the Desperate Dan strip in the *Beano* comic.

Sally bids goodnight, and I talk to the locals, who apart from cursory nods have not spoken thus far. Soon I am engaged in conversation with two fellows. One, with short cropped black hair, is in his late twenties but looks older. He works for the rural fire service. The other is his senior in years, and is keen to talk about farming.

A woman arrives and places a glass jar on the counter. Inside are two dead, hairy, spiders. They look to me like deadly Funnel Webs, or they could be (moderately) harmless Huntsmen. Regardless, she wants them identified, and leaves them on the counter for the barmaid and I to inspect.

A much older character steps across the threshold and joins in at the bar. He wears a hat, is unshaven, and is completely barefoot. The soles of his crusty feet are black with dirt, and his ankles are caked in dry, greying mud. The bar maid queries why he is such a mess and reaches for the mop she has on hand in the corner.

"I've been out with the heifers," he says.

Consulting with the regulars, who speak for me, and sort introductions—he finds out that I am a new jackeroo. He walks out to his ute and returns and shows me a tin of dubbin, and two pairs of good quality, woollen socks. He explains I must keep my feet dry at all costs, and that applying dubbin to the seams of my paddock boots will work wonders for their waterproofing properties. He pushes them into my hands.

"Here you go, these are yours," he says.

I thank him and wonder about his own feet as he singularly lacks footwear of any description.

"I tell you what, mate. Come and help me tomorrow morning, and I'll teach you."

"You'll learn more than on that farm," says one of the others.

The farmer says he will wake me at 4am, and then I can help him drive his cattle down the road to the highway. By now I am two sheets to the wind as the locals have been plying me with coke and rum mixes all night. I ponder this new offer of employment. Sally is sound asleep and will be bright-eyed and bushy-tailed tomorrow morning. I am decidedly non-committal.

I sleep fitfully, dreaming of early-morning wake-up calls, sheep and cattle. Every sound from outside wakes me (is it the farmer climbing up the fire escape to collect me?)

***

I rise at 8am and walk out the door on to the balcony of the fire escape outside my room. From here I can survey the town: there's the Emporium, and a disused railway line which cuts thought the adjoining lawn. After a bit of a wander, I find breakfast served in the back room. Sally pops up and we help ourselves to toast and cereal. James arrives, and we chuck our gear in the back of his ute.

The drive to the farm is only about 45 minutes. Cornelia Farm is heralded by a large sign. This is a 2,500 acre cattle property, running mostly cattle ("Droughtmaster" James says.) The home is a classic long ranch-style one-storey build with a verandah under drooping metal eaves to protect against sub-tropical storms. We are met by Tom, and led through private rooms and out on to decking which runs the entire length of the homestead. Pensive backpackers prefer small talk thinking ahead to what's in store.

Tom, the owner, is an ex-Army Royal Engineers Colonel, and loses himself in an amusing rundown on his career, naming postings to exotic places. Backpackers smirk at his bumbling, retired army officer manner. An anecdote is cut short when his wife announces she will call us into the study to be allocated a farm.

Sally and I are put together with another English girl called Samantha. She is about 18 or 19, cherubic with a blonde bob, and wears a smart checked red shirt, a member of the Officer Training Corps back home. She is quite well-spoken, and gives the impression of being a know it all. I mentally call her "Two Shit Tyler", as for every crap someone says they have had, she's had two.

Tom's wife says the three of us are going out to Brickwood with Andrew and Helen, a farm down the road. As Brickwood doesn't use motorbikes, we will spend the afternoon here getting to grips with agricultural bikes under the tutelage of James. Tom ruffles his hair and adds Andrew used to be a pilot: we can talk flying.

Before lunch, we browse back issues of *Outback* magazine, a glossy bi-monthly publication which is full of supplements for RM Williams and equestrian outfitters, and has features on cattlemen and women (picked for their looks evidently). Served up is plates of salad, cold cuts, and juice by the live-in Dutch cook.

The first of the farmers arrive and pick up their students. Some are rude, and brusque, and cajole their poor backpackers along to their waiting utes. Someone is missing, and needs to be found, and the owner looks at their watch impatiently. I suppose you have to be cruel to be kind.

James calls us to follow him outside to get acquainted with Ag bikes: he has them lined up and starts with the essentials: we must be careful releasing the clutch or—

"You'll be doing wheelies!" he says, grinning. "Brakes–slow down with your foot, on the back brake–then come to a stop with the front." He points to the handlebars.

He sends us out to practise in the paddock. We sort of look like a motorbike display team as we circle around. When James deems we've grasped things, he sends us further afield, and I lead the way down a steep descending path in to a dried-up stream bed and then—full throttle—up the other side.

Andrew has arrived. He is aged about 50 and is sitting on a step dividing the study in two. He holds a battered cotton hat between his fingers. He is a slight man of medium height, with a twinkle in his eye, and a kindly expression. He shakes my hand and nods at me, and grabs a strap of a backpack when we hoist our gear into the Land Rover outside, before heading back on to the highway.

Andrew turns off a track lined by trees.

The farm is in a little fertile valley and the homestead is surrounded by towering trees. There's a flat, but sloping paddock to one side with a large pond, or dam. The homestead is two-storey brick construction with an open garage under the roofline. There's another Land Rover parked inside and Andrew kills the engine alongside it.

"Brickwood! 1,200 acres," he announces. "We run cattle, mostly Bradfords."

Sally spots pigs and chickens in a side yard next to a garden with exotic native plants.

"It looks like a children's petting school," she says.

A petite woman comes out and introduces herself as Helen. She introduces us to Justin, her 18-year-old son, and then looks around for her daughter, Abigail, 14, who pulls up on a John Deere tractor. She is typical of an Australian farm-raised schoolchild. She is barely five feet tall, but has a confidence and bearing of a woman in her twenties. She greets us with steely blue eyes, and a confident, almost defiant, expression. This schoolgirl would make light work of rounding up cattle with her father.

We head up climbing past wall-mounted bookcases on the stairs, into a wood-panelled living area. On the dresser, there is a picture of Andrew's plane. Helen asks us what kind of food we eat.

"I'm a Vegetarian," Sally says. Helen smiles.

"What are you going to do on a property?"

She's got a point. Meat is a staple on farms and stations.

They're not places where a person can be fussy about diet.

"You'll just have to make do, eh?"

Helen has a habit of saying "ay" at the end of her sentences, a habit many country Queenslanders have. As in "Might go into town tomorrow, ay?"

"I know," Sally says, with an expectant air; she has obviously already contemplated it. I hope future employers are sympathetic to her cause. Dinner is not quite there, so there is a job we can do first:

Justin and a jackeroo helper, who lives on the farm, are off in the field baling hay, so Abigail is going to take us out in the Land Rover to visit them so we can see what is involved. Outside the back door, looking for our boots, we are hit by swarms of mosquitoes. There are cans of Aerogard around, so we spray our arms and neck, and apply it to our faces. There's an old saying —"there's a time in every Australian's life when you realise the Aerogard is worse than the flies".

We drive over in the dark to the paddock. Abigail parks the Land Rover at the edge of the field and kills the engine but leaves the sidelights on to illuminate the scene. Justin and the live-in jackeroo are standing on the back of a truck pulling the baler. Andrew at the wheel is following a path of scythed wheat spiralling the paddock. The wheat is drawn up and packed in to blocks which drop out of a chute. One of the boys catches it, and swings it to the other, who is neatly stacking bails on the truck's flat bed.

The only sounds are the rhythmic baler and the trundling, idle of the truck. The night sky is jet-black and unspoilt by city lights. The stars are iridescent and bright, and the swirl of the milky way is clearly visible above us. The Southern Cross is as memorable in the south as the North Star Polaris is to the north. Abigail points to a nearby huge bank of stars.

"See the Hen?" she asks.

We gaze upwards but cannot recognise it. After coaching, we can see it ourselves. She's right. It's magnificent. It is made up of the constellations *Ophiuchus* and *Serpens* visible in the southern hemisphere winter. We go into dinner and sit to eat and chat. The TV is on, tuned to the Queensland news, and Samantha tells us all about her life in Fulham, London. She's quite talkative. After a while, the boys excuse themselves and go off in to the dark to shoot cane toads with Justin's .22 rifle.

CHAPTER 5 GETTING THE HANG OF IT

In the morning, I find I have overslept and have no time to dally. I dress, grab my hat, and race up the stairs to the dining room for breakfast to find Andrew sitting alone with Samantha. She greets me with a smug grin.

"Morning Steve. Don't worry, we've fed the chickens and the horses."

I could kill her. Luckily, Andrew looks unperturbed, and besides, Sally has yet to surface. I grab a bowl of cornflakes and pour myself a pot of tea, finding time to butter a few slices of bread. Sally emerges. Samantha is still talking to Andrew, and it looks like he is getting it in the ear.

We follow Andrew outside to a large tractor hitched to a hay trailer, and he explains we are going to feed cattle. He shows us the handbrake, the use of the clutch and gears and then asks Samantha to drive first. She is confident, I grant that, and trundles to a nearby fence where hungry cows have congregated. We drop the hay bundles into feed bins, tearing off sheets and throwing them over. A few land off-target, so I dive over the fence to reposition them.

Next stop is the goats. As we go past the homestead, which has a "bull nose" verandah, we can see a garden pond out the front which we haven't noticed before. A sloping track runs past outbuildings, continuing for a good half a kilometre. This turns out to be the runway, where Andrew operated a twin piston-engined aircraft. There's also a crayfish pond.

When we get back, Abigail is in the kitchen with a new arrival who is her governess. On the curriculum today: baking, and chocolate cakes cool on a rack. Helen has morning tea out on the front veranda, and the table is laden with iced tea, water and orange juice, cakes, biscuits. I can't believe it. We were here to be worked hard in a teaching setup, but we're also being looked after. Morning tea seems even archaic and conjures up images of Edwardian ladies drinking Earl Grey and eating cakes off lace doilies—it's not a phrase I've heard in London recently. The TV is on, and Kasey Chambers is singing "Not Pretty Enough".

Although we haven't finished the course, we have already registered ourselves on the list that is sent out to prospective employers. They get a pen-picture and profile of us and we can choose to cold-call them. Many people have jobs already. Sally gets an offer at a stables in Picton, Sydney, looking after horses, and taking children for rides, Samantha gets the governess job she was looking for.

Out the back, I admire an old ute belonging to Justin. It is a six-cylinder 1983 Holden "WB" utility and is the last of the line of Holden cars which originated in the early 1970s. It is bedecked with huge bull bar, spot lights, and a Castlemaine "4XXXX" beer poster adhered to the back window. It looks like the car from the cartoon *Dangermouse*, and is the same model as the vehicle I spied the day before yesterday. I ask him about the design.

"Great cars. They made them so well most are still running 30 years on. They were pretty much over-engineered," he says.

These utes are an Australian icon, and I can see why. Today, the Holden Commodore utility—in standard guise, or in full blown "sports" mode—competes with the Ford. If asked, most Australians will have a preference for either Holden or Ford. In fact, whole friendships and probably marriages are based on little else. At "B and S" (Bachelor and Spinster) parties out in the bush, people meet to run circles in paddocks and to find the best "beaut ute"—a whole culture has grown up. There's even a song about it—"Rootin' in the back of a ute".

"In the arvo, we're going riding," says Abigail.

"Arvo?" I question.

"Afternoon," she confirms.

Abigail is going to supervise the riding and we join her out the front amongst the chickens and the pigs. Sally admires my half chaps. Abigail has caught a horse or two already, but invites me to collect mine, a grey called Magic, which is standing in the paddock.

I have been riding on and off for years, and part of that experience has included sustained gallops, where I managed an air of competency. Catching horses and tacking them up, though, is a worry. At riding schools there were always plenty of people around to assist, so, I'm feeling self-conscious when I duck under the fence, and approach Magic. But nothing to worry about here—I slip the head collar over his neck.

We mount and ride out of the homestead and down the track to a tree-lined glade. Andrew is waiting there, dressed in his familiar Worzel Gummidge hat, and wants us to put our horses through their paces to assess our ability. Initially, he has us walking around the trees, performing figures of eight, and then he calls:

"Ok. Let's get these horses going!"

We spur our horses into a slow trot and I'm finding my seat awkward and I'm not looking great as I try to rise to the trot. I adjust my stirrups and he beams and says,

"Now you've got it."

I think we've all passed some sort of basic test.

Abigail leads us away out into the bush, and we leave Brickewood behind for a ride-out.

On the way back, the horses hold their heads high, strutting for the home straight, and Abigail turns around at the front of the ride and announces that we gallop back to the homestead. She takes off, and we need no second bidding. With one kick, Magic is off, and gains on Samantha, who is ahead of me. They are running neck and neck, and I go from my controlled, collected canter, to a forward seat. As we approach the homestead, I glance back to see Sally bringing up the rear, and look forward again, just in time to see a tree. The path to the homestead runs in both directions around it, so I'm not bothered which side we take. I rein back, but Magic whips me dangerously close to the tree, bucking away at the last moment.

Abigail laughs.

"He always does that."

As the light fades, we use what's light is left in the paddock to finish the baling. The three of us get on the truck, and under the watchful eyes of Justin, stack the bales as they emerge from the baler. There's a trick to stacking the bales—it's a game of Tetris on a Gameboy.

As an Australian homestead is essentially a working home, they are invariably rustic and simple, furnished without pretension and cozy. Many houses have a games room where no money has been spared to create a personalised room for the family. This is often used to entertain guests and would probably be the first room a guest would see upon being ushered in through the front door.

We won't miss out with a full-sized pool table. Justin is watching an evening live NRL game from ANZ Stadium,which his team, the Brisbane Broncos, is playing in. A quick scan of the videos on the shelf above the television reveal *Coyote Ugly*— Abigail's favourite film.

At dinner, I get talking to Andrew about flying, and he promises to find his copy of the old classic, *Stick and Rudder*.

"Just remember where the ground, is, Steve," he says.

***

It's all hands on deck the next day. We head back to Cornelia, as they need our help with a cattle muster. Helping your neighbours is a key trait in country Australia. James is awaiting us, along with others from the course, and in no time at all, we are readying the horses. He briefs us on what we can expect this afternoon. We will ride over to a river and muster any cattle we find out there, returning by another route. It will be easy-going, and the only need to push the pace is when a mob break away from the main herd.

It takes us a good part of an hour to get to the river system and we have quite a head of cattle by then. It is slow, and at times, boring work. It's not like what you might see on TV.

The terrain opens back out into plains, and we split into pairs, and escort the cattle on the left flank, right, or directly behind. Two riders are sent to scout out any dead or high ground that may conceal cattle that have wandered off. The route passes through moderately dense, sloping woodland.

We come across the occasional head of cattle grazing in the shade of eucalypt trees. Andrew scurries to and fro, up to each pair passing on tips. When our turn comes, he talks to me about mustering with aircraft, flicking flies out of his face with his free hand—the "Aussie salute".

Back at the farm, we drove the muster into a large holding pen which abuts a series of complicated looking races, seven feet high. Sally gets off her horse to help a calf through a gate, and Samantha says:

"Do you think we should be getting off, is it safe?"

These pen systems are known as races, whereby the operation of doors and gates, and quick-witted thinking, cattle can be filtered. We dismount, and Andrew takes us through the theory. He explains we need to work smoothly, and quietly, too, as we do not want to excite the herd any more than necessary. He warns us to watch out for being crushed against the side of a pen, and that a gate doesn't get slammed shut on an arm or a leg. (Both ours, and theirs.)

We are hoping to separate out the mob by age and sex, and then ear-tag, brand, and de-horn, and castrate the calves. James gestures at me to get in the pen with the cattle to assist the droving. I drop in, feeling at once vulnerable knowing full-well several hundred kilos of beef would have the upper hand in any stampede. I hang back near the side, taking care not to get underfoot.

When the inner pen is full, we close the gate. As James is closing it, a steer runs through and unwittingly, he pushes the bolt through its hide; it lets out an agonising bellow. Samantha and Sally look away in disgust.

We locate a male calf and entice it in to one of the races, closing gates behind it. With our hats, we cajole it down the race and in to the trap. The trap swivels on its side exposing the calf's hind legs and rear quarters. There's a branding iron connected to a car battery. James asks me to hold the calf's legs apart, and he applies the iron. I see smouldering and smell scorched flesh — and hear a bellow. Well, wouldn't you shout? James whips out his leatherman, and cuts into the calf's testicles, flicking each out, throwing them to the dogs. On cue, Samantha bends forward and tags the ear with the correct tag, which causes the calf to squeal once more. The calf staggers over to its mother.

We swap over roles for the next. When given the nod by James, I press the branding iron into the flesh.

"Harder. You need to hold the burn," James says. I press more firmly and am rewarded by the scorched smell again.

"OK, that's fine."

After our meal, I show an interest in what has been so far a evening ritual: the boys' nocturnal shooting party. Night arrives sooner here than down south. I find Justin and his mate in a huddled conference. Justin has a .22 rifle in hand, and his mate is examining several boxes of ammunition with which he is going to keep him supplied. This is clearly a favourite time—two blokes on a station. I join them, and they register my presence but largely ignore me; this does not bother me as they seem content to talk together in a lampooning country lingo they have adopted for this little spree.

Cane toads are an epidemic in Queensland. Nasty and ugly, they are a pest, yet they were originally introduced intentionally as a natural predator against rats. They solved that problem, but the toad population exploded. Australia has a long history in introducing species in an endless battle against undesirables, only to find that the introduced then becomes a new problem in a crazy pattern of survival of the fittest.

At the crayfish ponds, I can see in the moonlight that tens of toads are out in the grass on the banks waiting to feed. Justin loads, and still chuckling, takes aim in the shoulder, and with a loud accompanying crack, the toad topples over. The boys both burst into laughter. Justin kicks the toad in to the pond and renews aim. In perhaps a minute, eight toads have been dispatched into the water, and, we are off round the pond's perimeter searching for new targets. The live-in jackeroo also has a torch which he swings around search-light style; Justin follows the beam with the muzzle of the weapon—they make a good team. He spots a huge bird sat by the side of the pond. In a cloud of feathers, it is likewise dispatched, and this sends the boys in to fits of giggles.

I reckon they have shot at least 200 toads, so I leave them to it.

***

Andrew is going to introduce us to irrigation. Is this taps, piping, head pressure, flow rates and sprinklers? It would have to be hard work if we're involved.

He drives us down in a spare bleached Land Rover to the bottom paddock. We spy a long line of pipes about twice the diameter of a scaffolding pole. Andrew says that he wants us to shift the entire pipeline 20 metres. As the sections are heavy, the trick is to find the centre of gravity, before lifting. Samantha keeps up a long-running commentary; she's annoying.

Andrew has a little trick: divining for water. He holds two rods in his hands, and advances to where he knows there is water. The rods swing from pointing directly forwards, to sideways. So far, so good. With a smirk on his face, he jogs up and down on the spot counting to himself.

"12 metres down," he announces.

When I look doubtful, he indicates the end of the field, and I look over the fence to a water course running alongside. Sure enough, it's about 12 metres down. I get it though, I think he is having us on.

Breaking for lunch, Abigail gets out a Uno deck which is easy to play—however, true to form, I am slow to pick up the rules, and whilst Sally and Samantha are content to roll their eyes at my stupidity, Abigail rewards my intransigence by thumping me resoundingly on the arm.

We head back out to handle stock. A cow escapes and stampedes up the paddock, and in an impressive display of horsemanship, Abigail—14 years old remember—gallops up the paddock after it, barefoot, and bareback.

"She's an incredible horsewoman, isn't she?" Sally says.

Most of the cattle are already processed, but Andrew wants to separate those that need de-horning. We catch a young male in the trap, and Andrew grabs a pair of cutters and scissors through the horns. Sally looks away as blood squirts out, and Andrew, noticing, looks up and says:

"It's an animal, Sally! Those horns will cost me dollars per kilogram."

It's the first time I have seen Andrew look peeved.

We try our hand at mending fences, a real skill on a station. It's a useful skill on a large station as it is often necessary to build a makeshift paddock for stock during a long muster. The idea is to splice two lengths of wire under tension, using a kind of ratchet device. Get it wrong, as both Sally and I did, and the ends ping apart, and you have to start again. Annoyingly, Samantha gets it right first time. The sun is slipping fast, and a band of the blue sky has turned to a beautiful purple, with the rest a golden glow. The paddocks appear lush, and we stand for a moment at the side of the paddock and admire the breathtaking view.

At dinner, Samantha is talkative, and tells us about her life once again in London. Sophie Ellis-Bextor is on television with "Murder on the Dance floor", and Samantha says casually they were both at school together. When she announces she once attended a function at the Royal Albert Hall, I can't resist a little joke.

"So, who were you hob-nobbing with this time?" I comment.

There is a brief silence as Sally smirks. Helen has a titter momentarily. Samantha doesn't notice and carries on talking.

Abigail invites us out to look for possums in the Land Rover, her grubby feet barely reaching the pedals. I sit next to her, and the girls jump in the back. Abigail slows to a crawl, and cranes her neck upwards, looking for the reflective eyes of possums in the trees.

***

On the last day, as we pack, Andrew comes by, and announces that Justin has found rats in the sheds. We go over to find him with his .22, walking around the shed, rifle at the ready. He climbs up, balancing precariously on a wooden plank, and inserts his rifle barrel into the pipe and sends two rounds in. *Crack! Crack!* It seems to do the trick, because when he upends the pipe, two rats fall out the end on to the floor.

We load up the Land Rover with our gear and say farewell. Sally is quite sad to leave, and she has a few sniffles when she hugs Helen goodbye.

"Come back any time you like. You're welcome here. Not like that other girl. God. She never shut up."

Back at Cornelia, we have half an hour to discuss the course with the other groups. They found it hard work, and sometimes found the hosts rude. One of the lads wipes his brow and says:

"Yeah–we were kept at it all day. We couldn't do anything right."

Sally mentions the luxury of our morning teas and their eyes widen with amazement and envy. By comparison, thanks in part to Andrew's laid-back nature, we had an easy time of it. Samantha is still yacking away.

We fold into our seats on the coach at Goomeri, waiting to head back to Brissy and review our week together, discussing the highs and the lows. We are both unanimous in that Andrew and Helen could not have been better hosts. Another graduate hangs over her seatback and paints a less rosy picture of the course, complaining of her brusque hosts. She has, however, got a job with a polo team, and is excited as there will be a fair amount of travel involved.

"The boss sounds a bit of a prick, though," she counters.

In Brisbane, that night, we connect with the bus continuing down south to Sydney. The journey is an 18-hour trip, and so we will drive through the entire night, arriving in Sydney around lunch. As the night progresses, we freeze on the bus. Backpackers go forward and ask the coach driver to "turn off the AC" but there's nothing he can do. I'm glad I got my sleeping bag.

CHAPTER 6 THE POMMY JACKEROO

"So, can you tell me a bit about the job?" I ask Bronwyn, speaking clearly on the phone, from a backpackers on Kent Street, located in the CBD on Sydney.

Bronwyn explains the job to me. The job involves sheep—ie bikes, not horses—on a rural station in New South Wales, operated by Bronwyn and Glen, her husband. I will be paid 100 bucks a day, will get a free cottage next to the homestead, and as much free eggs and lamb chops as I can eat. (I have a list of potential job offers on a yellow stick-it note, and this is the second number I have called.)

"So, you'll take the job, then?" she asks.

The work sounds like what I am after though, and the offer is good. I decide on the spot.

"Yes, I'll accept. When can I start?" I ask.

"OK. We're shearing next week, after Easter. Can you come up for that? Shearing starts Wednesday. Glen can collect you from the coach stop."

It sounds feasible. I leave the TV room and wait in the corridor for an old, clanking lift.

Sally leaves for her job, and I give her a massive hug when she leaves me. I'm sad to see her go, as we seem to have come through quite a lot this last week.

"See you later, Steve–take care!" she says.

My station is Buckton station, near Walgett, north-central rural New South Wales, not far from the Queensland border. It is not quite as remote as other places in the state; Bourke, the real gateway to the outback—once you are "back of Bourke" you are "outback"—is still a good 300 miles away almost due West.

I travel by train on the CountryLink XPT which departs Sydney Central early Tuesday and arrives in Dubbo, in south-central New South Wales in the afternoon. Here I change to a coach which, after a trawl north, arrives in Walgett in the early evening. Covering 22,000 square kilometres, Walgett Shire is one of the largest local government areas in the State.

***

Walgett (pop: 3,000) turns out to be bigger than a one-horse town with a single main street running past a supermarket and several clubs and hotels. It has banks, a credit union, and a general store. It hasn't rained in this part of the state for the best part of the year and the region is dry. I am standing at the bus stop, by a municipal park where groups of indigenous children play.

There's a supermarket on a corner, so I decide to buy supplies before Glen turns up. The supermarket looks like a shop in an Eastern European country in past days under Communism. It sells the main staples and not much else.

A white rusty Toyota Land Cruiser pulls up in the main road, and I wave speculatively. This will be the start of a long relationship I will develop with this type of vehicle, this year. I squint through the windscreen at a figure sitting alone behind the wheel. From his reaction, I assume that the figure is Glen. He steps out and says "G'Day." He is about six foot four, in his early forties, and wears a wide-brimmed Akubra. He is stoutly built, though not running to athleticism nor fat. He has a grizzly red beard and piercing green eyes.

I throw my gear on the back of his ute, and we set off. He has to visit the bottle shop drive-in, so I order a slab of Tooheys. As we drive back down the main street of Walgett, Glen, as is to be expected, knows everyone in town and raises his finger off the steering wheel at pretty much everybody. Occasionally, he will call out a greeting, or stop and have a yarn to someone he feels deserves particular attention.

We turn off the main street and on to a wide, dirt track. Glen picks up speed.

After half an hour, we arrive at the property in the dark—no stars tonight—and pull up at a gate composed of two stout beams. We pass through, and I can see lights presumably from the homestead to my left. The Cruiser's lights illuminate a smaller wooden cottage to the right.

"This is where you'll be Steve," he says.

I step out into the gloom and grab my rucksack off the back of the tray. Glen leads me through a gate up the path to the cottage, throwing on lights as he steps inside.

"Leave your gear, please, Steve."

I chuck my gear down, and lower the slab on to the floor, and follow him back outside, not having time to see my digs.

We get back in the Land Cruiser, and this time, the headlights pick out a much larger shed. Glen leads again. I can see at once this is the shearing shed and we are in an entrance anteroom. In front of us is a table, with offcut bins beside it, and my novice eye picks out wool racks.

There's a mob of sheep in system of fenced pens waiting to be sheared. The pens connect to about six small empty pens, each of which has a gate leading to a narrow strip of floor. I can see this is where the shearers will stand.

Glen walks out amongst the sheep, and the sheep back up away from him against the far fence.

"Help me Steve, I am going to get them inside," he says.

He faces towards me, and walks backwards, saying "swish" as he does, and waving his arms around like he is trying to take off.

"See the way I am starting at the front, Steve," he says. I nod and join him. The sheep run past us—true to form, once one sheep goes, others follow.

"OK good," he says, satisfied. "Remember that."

We get back in the idling Land Cruiser, losing our night-vision in the headlights. We drive over to the homestead and pull up in the yard, and Glen leads me down a path to the side door. We enter a wooden-floored annexe which leads through into the combined kitchen and living room. Bronwyn is there by the table, serving dinner.

"G'Day Steve. How are you going?" she says.

"Good thanks," I say, mindful of the protocol required.

There is another man, here, aged in his late fifties or early sixties. He is silently sitting at the dining table, with a plate chewing silently, staring into space. He's come to assist tomorrow. He appears to be a vital personality in tomorrow's shearing. Glen sits next to him.

I'm placed next to Bronwyn, facing the television which for the moment, is off, and like a conjuror, she produces a plate of lamb chops and veggies from somewhere and passes me a dripping jug of gravy. I am hungry after my day's travelling, and tuck in.

I listen to the conversation: Glen and the new man, who turns out to be Roger, are discussing a computer printout of figures and graphs, and it appears they are talking about wool prices and stock. I look at them inquisitively. The conversation is one-sided, Glen is engrossed in talking, and the man is silently listening, sipping a cup of tea whilst gripping the paper in his other hand. Occasionally, with a grubby thumb, Glen points out a figure or two.

"Roger, now look here," he says. Roger glances up from a mouthful.

"So–prices are up Roger, we're looking at 20 good ones a kilo right now in Woolies."

"Righto," he observes.

Bronwyn notices me leaning forward, and interrupts.

"Well, are you going to tell Steve a bit about what is going on?"

I smile and look interested.

I excuse myself and pick my way back to my workers' cottage for an inspection.

There's a little lobby with a bench worn smooth by countless backsides. Taking off my yard boots, and picking up the slab of beer, I manoeuvre through the interior door, into a small kitchen, with table, chairs, and refrigerator, and electric stove. I set down the slab on the dog-eared lino.

A door leads through into a modest living room, furnished with a tatty sofa and a television set (which doesn't work.) Wooden floor boards are offset by a threadbare carpet. On the back wall is a door leading outside—*alfresco* dining? Another door leads into a bedroom, which has a double bed, with comfy looking bedclothes, and a substantial dresser with mirror.

I throw my pack onto the bed and go out the back. Apart from outbuildings in the distance, I can see nothing else apart from a clothesline and an annexe to my left. Gingerly stepping across the dusty concrete, I enter the annexe and find the combined bathroom and laundry. Here is a shower, a toilet, and a top-loader washing machine hooked up to a rusty industrial sink. (Front-loader automatics are not so popular "Down Under"— they are considered an European contrivance.)

I strip off and jump in the shower stepping over bugs and brushing away cobwebs: the plumbing hums and thunders, the water tepid.

***

I rise, shave quickly and get dressed in my work clobber. I peer outside, and now I can see my new workplace. My cottage, with the shearing shed nearby, faces the homestead across a dirt yard, which is also a natural road and access area to the shed. The road continues past the shed to the rest of the property one way, and the other direction is the entrance to the property which we drove through last night.

Due to the drought, the vegetation is sparse, save for the occasional blade of grass, and the ground for hundreds of metres around is dry, cracked dirt. It's quite a sombre sight.

I stand in front of the dresser and conscientiously apply Factor 30 sunblock to my face and neck, and to the bit of exposed chest where my shirt buttons. Breakfast is toast which I have with Bronny who is now dressed in a baby-blue denim shirt.

"Steve," she cautions: "Forgot to say–keep your kitchen clean– food attracts rats and rats attract snakes–here's a bin."

I make sure I have my water bottle, a hat, leatherman tool, and make my way over to the shearing shed for eight o'clock. The sun, although low, sits in a cloudless sky, and I seek the shade. Glen comes over and says "Good Morning". He disappears somewhere.

The shearers arrive in the back of a troop carrier, and finding themselves a station, prepare their tools. They are wearing shorts, paddock boots and "Jackie Howe" singlets. These are named after a famous shearer who still holds the Australian record for the number of sheep sheared in a single session— 321 sheep in 7 hours, 40 minutes on 10th October 1892, at Alice Downs, Queensland. Jackie started the practise of wearing a singlet when he tore the sleeves of his flannel undershirt.

They are paid by the number they shear in four, two-hourly runs, thus creating competition to get the largest tally for the day. The fastest and cleanest shearer for the day's tally earns for himself the name the "Ringer of the Shed". Roger from last night is standing by the classification table: as wool classer, his job is to grade the wool and place it in the correct bin as he sees fit—and the shearers change into moccasins for comfort.

I act as the "tar boy", the jackeroo who traditionally would bring over the tar used to stop bleeding. This practice is no longer employed, but I will be there to sweep and pack down the wool bales and to attend.

At 8:30 sharp, for the first run of the day, one of the shearers presses a button, and with a shrill, the mechanical pulleys and cogs in the ceiling rotate and power the mechanical blades of the shearers' tools. Each shearer advances forward to collect a sheep from the pen opposite them. They cradle it and shear off its wool using a methodical process that has not changed in centuries.

I watch with interest as the shearers complete their first sheep, all finishing neck and neck. The sheep are allowed out between their legs through holes in the shed, into pens outside. I sweep up the scrags—the useless offcuts and help gather the wool on to the table.

I get talking to one of the shearers closest to me, and whilst he shears, he can keep up a limited dialogue. He is a well-built man, about 50, with a mop of unruly hair and missing teeth that show every time he grins broadly, which is often. The back of his neck is rudely burnt, the sort that he wouldn't notice but would hurt like hell for most.

Glen arrives and asks me to clean out the outhouses I saw from the back of my cottage, handing me a broom.

"Sweep out the dunnies, please Steve," he asks.

"Just make sure all the spider's webs and crap are cleared away," he adds agreeably.

The outhouses turn out to be the shearer's dunnies (toilets). I have been given worse tasks, and so I open the first dunny and start. As they have not been used for a while, it is not unpleasant and there are no nasty whiffs or repellent smells. When I enter the second outhouse, I sanguinely look around to gauge the job in hand, and am back outside the dunny in a flash:

I have just seen a Redback spider, that most insidious and dangerous of Australian arachnopods. It is, without doubt, a Redback: it has a red speck on its back—a female of the species —and is barely larger than my big thumb's thumbnail. Yet a single bite from its poisoned fangs, whilst probably not killing an adult, will almost certainly hospitalise me. It would make my eyes water, put it that way.

Crouched against the dunny, I figure my next move. I am reminded of clearing houses as a young paratrooper on exercise in my late teens. A section of us would stand outside a house prior to entry, and a man would be chosen to make his entry— through a door or a window:

I stand up and straighten, pause, and with broom in hand, rush through the door and crush the redback to a pulp, aggressively and forcefully. It's a while before I work out this was overkill, but needs must.

Bronwyn comes over:

"Steve, we've got to get some sheep."

She explains a few things.

"That looks like a nice shirt. Is it a Calvin Klein shirt?" she asks, pointing at the label. "I've got old shirts you can have. You don't have to wear those."

I explain that it is an old shirt, and she nods. I've obviously given away my city ways and sensibilities.

"Nice watch though," she announces, leaning forward. It's an automatic Omega Stainless Steel dive watch—not only it is waterproof to 300m (now who would try) but designed with durability in mind—even remote locations out here in the bush —not that I had considered that when I bought it.

She leads me to a large shed containing a brace of Honda 250cc quad bikes, a dumpy child's bike, and a collection of tools and clobber. Bronwyn checks I have my Driz-a-Bone, a hat, a water bottle, and gives me a quick five-minute lesson on the Honda controls and indicates the fuel bowser where I can top up.

She straddles her bike, and we head off out of the main gate and tear off down the track. I speed faster and faster, fearful of being left behind. I hit a rut, and I careen off the dirt track on the grass verge, somehow coming to a halt in a cloud of dust. I get back on the dirt track and catch up without her noticing.

After reckless driving, we arrive in amongst a flock of sheep. Bronny indicates she wants me to help her drive them back to the shearing sheds. I am dazed and excited from the mad bike ride, so when some sheep dive off, I'm after them in a trace. The mob panics and splits. Bronny is screaming at me to calm down and go slower.

"Steve. Never split the flock like that!"

So, we take things a lot more slowly. She takes one side, and I take the rear. She steers them by alternating sides - my role is to propel them from the rear. We're very casual now—just a fast walking pace—it will take the best part of a few hours to get back to the sheds. Our job is made easier by a fence line which protects one of our flanks, so Bronny leaves her station and motors over.

"OK Steve, I'll leave them with you," and she roars off back to the homestead.

I continue to drove the mob. It is straight forward for a while, but I run in to difficulties.

Without Bronny on the far flank to keep them in check, recalcitrant members of the flock seize their chance to scarper. When I bring them back, the mob run the other way. No amount of droving will keep them going the right way. After an age of frustrating manoeuvring, I am starting to panic.

I see a figure on the bike coming back in my direction. It's Bronny.

"Where have you been?" she shouts above the engine noise. I shout my predicament.

"They won't go straight."

"Have you been rounding them in circles, Steve?"

I think I might have been. That would be accurate.

When we get back, shorn sheep are accumulating in the outside pens, and they require "drenching". Glen and I allow a mob to run into two narrow enclosures, and I survey the 50 or so sheep that have been trapped in one lane. I slip my arms through the straps of a canister of formula which I wear "backpack-style", and cradle a nozzle gun in my hand—designed to kill worm in sheep guts. I need to administer five cc to each sheep and Glen has already given me a demonstration. Suffice to say he was very quick.

I vault the pen fence and grab my first sheep. After a long struggle, I ram the gun down its throat and squeeze the trigger. A dose of liquid jets out of the side of its mouth.

Try again.

It's a small victory when I work out by trial how to position the nozzle in the sheep's mouth.

"Don't miss any, Steve. It's that important," insists Glen.

I go to the second sheep. Repeat process. After 20 minutes or so, I finish, breathing hard. I am streaked with pink from the sheep's cuts. The oil from what is left of the sheep's wool has seeped through my trousers and has created a Barbour wax-like sheen. Glen watched me finish up, and suggests if I pin down several sheep up against the run, I can reach them in batches, saving me time and energy.

He's right: I catch my first sheep and swing it around– by kicking its hindquarters with my foot—so that it blocks the width of the pen. It backs off into its fellows and they all jam tightly together. My knee pins its shoulders. I dose five with deliberate motions now they cannot move, then let that number through my legs. Occasionally, I turn around an extra sheep that is trying to flee through: a nudge to its withers, and it obliges.

The second batch of 50 sheep is easier. That's a start, as in total, I've got 2,000 to do, spaced over five days.

I jump back on my bike for another shift with Bronny and collect more sheep from another outlying paddock. We go through the gate leading to the rest of the property and approach a new paddock and Bronny announces that this is the "middle" paddock.

Well, bugger me, it looks just like all the others.

And what's more, the flies are a constant companion— my back is carpeted with them, they are everywhere seeking moisture. They arrive with the heat of the day and depart once the sun is low in the sky.

Once the sheep are secure for the night, and the bike refuelled, I am dismissed along with the shearers, who head off in their transport. In my digs, I kick off my yard boots and sink on to the tatty sofa, contemplating my first day. I grab a stubby of New out of the fridge and cut my finger on a bottle I placed in the freezer box to chill and forgot about, which has exploded. I suck my finger, fashion a torniquet and band-aid the wound.

CHAPTER 7 SETTLING IN

I'm getting the hang of droving sheep with Bronny. We're escorting a mob back to the paddocks and she comes roaring up to me on her bike, and I assume she is going to take me to task for some misdemeanour—but she shouts from underneath her hat:

"Now you're getting it!" and races off.

As we have a fair distance to go this morning, we find that the younger lambs are having difficulty keeping up. I pick one up. Bronny comes over and watches him, and he collapses, and loses consciousness. I place him sympathetically on the back of my quad bike. Minutes later, he slides off, his neck catching in the luggage rack; if he wasn't dead then, he is now. I look at Bronny, and she indicates a tree. I sling the body around the base of it, and we move on.

Casualties mount: back at the run, I find a sheep lying in the bottom of the pen, panting and severely dehydrated. It is losing blood from a nasty cut near its jugular where the shearer has cut too close. It dies too, though—and I throw the body out of the pen. Bronny peers at it, shrugs, and walks away. Later, I see Glen cutting it up with the band saw in the outhouse. The mutton will make good dog food.

Glen calls me to help organise sheep in the outside pens waiting to be sheared. We are basically moving them up closer to the shed. I am doing OK—moving quickly in and out of pens under Glen's tutelage. One sheep is left behind in a pen, and in trying to get away from me, runs at a closed gate—the wrong gate—as it happens, and collides into it.

"****ing Idiot!" Glen cries.

I'm not sure if he means me or the sheep.

Bronny turns up and gives us a hand: a large ram tries to bolt through a gate when we are selecting for ewes. She is using all her might to hold it back. I vault the fence and go to her aid. Another sheep is having difficulty in trying to squeeze through, although from the panicked look on its face I know it desperately wants to comply and follow its chums. Glen is trying to close the gate on it, but its foot is in the way, and he loses his temper and stamps on its leg until it snaps.

"That will teach you!" he screams.

I am shocked by this display—Glen has only just been lecturing me about not filling the pens too full.

I now need to send my flock back to the paddocks outside the homestead around the corner. I open the gate leading out to the rest of the property, and the gate to the holding pen. How to usher the sheep around? Glen tells me to stand in the strip of ground between the homestead and the holding area.

"Just stand there, please, Steve. By the tree."

I stand near the tree and face the holding pen. Glen swishes them out and they come running out towards me. I make swishing sounds myself, and *en masse* they turn on a sixpence and start streaming towards the gate in the paddock. I grin at this little hack. I was standing in exactly the right place.

*****

I am standing in the shearing shed out of the sun having a breather when Glen comes up—obviously in a rush. "Get your hat and come with me, please, Steve. Bring your water bottle." I notice this about Glen. He is curt, he is rude, but he still finds time to add a quick "please" to every request. I beat him to the Toyota, and hop in.

We head off in the usual direction of the middle paddock, going through all the paddocks this side of it. I go through my usual routine of—open gate—wait for the ute to pass through—go through myself—close gate—swing into ute. I've got it down to a fine art now. I can reach up, grab the handle above the door and be seated in the passenger seat, with the door closed, in one graceful movement. The Dukes of Hazzard would be proud. This does little to impress Glen.

As we drive the dirt track, a cloud of dust behind us, I keep an eye on the odometer. I'm finding it interesting establishing how far apart things are. For example, yesterday we drove 16 kilometres to find a lost calf. That's about ten miles. When I was at school, I used to cycle ten miles from our home in Twickenham, West London, to a friend's house in Ashford, further west—it would take me the best part of an hour and I would arrive tired and thirsty. Now Glen and I drive this routinely in between places to attend to minor jobs. I am getting this mental picture in my head for the layout of the farm although most of the paddocks look alike. The information will be useful if I am tasked to go alone somewhere on my bike.

After 20 minutes of silence, and me eyeing the odometer, we pull up at a mud oasis in the middle of nowhere. Three large sheep with winter coats, are embedded in the mud.

"Stupid ****!" Glen says.

He gets to work quickly, whilst I watch. He grabs a rope from the ute's tray and attempts to lasso a sheep, but he is too far away; his aim is not good. I spot cardboard on the tray and start laying it on the mud so he can stand closer. Glen offers no thanks, or acknowledgement, for this unsolicited display of initiative. He gets there in the end and snags one. I am thankful, because at every missed opportunity, he curses. The lasso tightens around the sheep's withers. He bends over and ties its back legs together, and one of its forelegs to these. With a full coat, and a muddy one at that, he needs my assistance, as it must weigh at least 60kg.

"Let's go," he grunts.

On three, we swing the sheep, and it lands in the back of the ute on the flatbed tray. The others are swung on to the back in similar fashion. In gaining a purchase on the last sheep's leg, I get a finger-full of spinifex—incredibly sharp Australian bush thorn. Without a word, Glen gets into the ute; I jump on the back to keep an eye on the sheep.

Glen tells me we are now off to catch two rams out in remote pens. When we arrive, the rams are backed in to a corner of a large pen with 6 ft high fenced walls. Glen stands at one side of the short side where the gate is, and I stand at the other. We pick a ram and advance slowly towards it. As we get closer, it backs off, and we close the net between us. I am right next to it. Glen says, very quietly:

"Get it, please, Steve."

In for a penny, in for a pound: I dive across and grab it firmly just behind the horns and plant my knee in its middle before it can bolt. Glen seems to momentarily be satisfied. We tie it up in the same manner and chuck it on the back of the ute. The second ram causes us problems. It charges past us, and I have a choice to tackle it head-on, and risk injury from its horns, or allow it to scamper past. A few times, I err on the side of caution, and it scampers past. Glen swears.

Back at the homestead, Glen invites me to knock off for the day as it is now dusk. I head off to my cottage, and Glen turns and walks across the dirt yard to the homestead.

***

As the fourth, and penultimate day of shearing falls on a Friday, I am hoping to go into town to grab a beer, after I have knocked off. I even mention it to the shearers at morning "smoko" (break), who have taken to calling me the "Pommy Jackeroo", and one, a half-aboriginal, sings it to himself, chuckling.

"Ah, yeah! You'll find plenty of 'Gins' down there, Pommy," laughs my mate.

When I look puzzled, he says:

"Local lasses, mate."

He then launches into a diatribe of chuckling about the merits of the local women, which he finds very funny. My mate wanders off and spends the next half an hour chuckling to himself, occasionally looking in my direction and laughing at his joke.

Whatever the motive, a beer and counter meal becomes more and more tempting as the day gets hotter and hotter. But it is not going to happen, as it becomes clear when tentatively I raise the subject with Glen.

"We're not going into town for at least another couple of weeks," he says.

I am crestfallen—a weekend alone in the cottage. I resume my work, sweeping out the wool in the shed.

I languish in my cottage most of the weekend enduring the solitude and the boredom. God knows how I keep occupied. I reach a height of boredom on Sunday afternoon:

I poke at my pet tree frog which I caught on Saturday. (It was lying in the middle of the bathroom when I walked in that morning.)

I alternate between the two channels on TV. (Glen brought the TV round at the weekend on the back of the quad bike.) I write out "top ten" lists. (Favourite music, favourite bands, favourite films, last ten girlfriends and their best quality et cetera.)

I cook. I re-read the trivia questions on the discarded Tooheys New bottle tops which lie in a mound on the counter, all of them.

I jog out of the station, and back again. (The appeal of exercise soon vanished.)

As a last resort, I even design and sketch imaginary computer systems on sheets of A4.

I think about what I could be doing.

I could be watching a game of footy in the sports bar, talking to, and lapping up the attention of a pretty, wide-eyed country girl, impressing her with my European sophistication. I am irritated that there are no girls to flirt with on the farm. Fantasies of rolling around in the hay, in the stables, will sadly never come to fruition. Finally, I ring up Sarah, who is having a trying time of it too on her farm. When I call, she is watching the *Wizard of Oz*. I flick it on. I explain Glen's crankiness, which I can live with, and how it looks like I am going to have very little social interaction, which frankly I can't. She doesn't particularly like her job, as the girls are rather bitchy—seemingly an insular bunch.

***

The new week brings with it the last day of shearing. The largest sheep are a real handful—but I am also more skilled and can still manage a steady pace. The Merinos are last—the rams look like small majestic ponies as befits their world-renowned wool. A local vet has turned up to take blood samples and he will need my assistance in holding them. As I pin one against the race, scrummaging like an international prop, Bronwyn comes up and says "G'Day" to the vet. She notices me alongside:

"Oh Steve, you're invited over to the homestead this evening for dinner, seeing as today's the last day."

Dinner. At the homestead. I've got a social life. Well, that's decided—I'm going—and there's no need to consult my diary. We finish up: Glen offers me a beer in a stubbie and the shearers stand around.

The evening turns out to be an amusing one. We have a fantastic meal, of lamb—it's not exactly in short-supply here as you can imagine—and veggies, followed by one of my favourites, a rich rice pudding, just in time for the Queen Mother's funeral broadcast from Westminster Abbey. Glen and Bronwyn are absorbed by proceedings and watch with interest, making the occasional comment. I'm impressed to see they can identify most of the Royals as they arrive and process into the Abbey. I've noticed the number of back issues of *Australian Women's Weekly* lying around which contain lots of articles and photos of the Royals: the Queen still sits as head of the Commonwealth of which Australia is part. When I ask after the identity of an obscure Royal, Glen says:

"You're the Pom, mate. You'd have a better idea surely." I raise the subject of when Prime Minister Paul Keating infamously put his arm around the Queen when she visited Australia in the early 1990s. Glen reckons it was a "that way, Marm" gesture

and that although he didn't like Keating as a "pollie", he was
sympathetic as Keating was viciously ridiculed for breaching
Royal protocol, labelled as the "Lizard from Oz". He carries on
this vein for a while, and seems to get stuck in a rut until Bronny
says:

"Do you ever shut up Glen?"

***

With shearing over, I am given a "day off", mowing the
homestead's back lawn and I put in neat lines, snaking around
Bronny and the Hills Hoist—a reputable brand of washing line.
She leans over, hand on knee and winds on a handle and the
sodden laundry is hoisted up into a light breeze coming off the
paddocks.

"Steve, got to wash Jim's sheets. That's my boy–he's at Joeys."

St Joseph's is a well-known private boys' school in Sydney, an
elite boarding school admitted to the GPS— Great Public School
ranking. It's sort of the Ivy league of the Australian secondary
school system where boys take their High School Certificate at
18. It's common for farming families to send their boys and girls
away for school, yet return to marry and take over the farm.

After the panic of shearing, it seems pedestrian.

The following afternoon, I start "pig-sticking". What's that?
Clearing dead wood from the paddock—six miles from home
with nothing but my bike, a trailer, and a water bottle for
company.

Glen explains I must zig-zag in lanes in the paddock, picking
up large pieces of wood. The job seems simple enough, but I
soon encounter little problems that prove to be an annoyance.
The paddock is so big and featureless, I have problems driving
in a straight line from one side of it to another. I line up a tree
on the perimeter a mile away, but then after stopping to pick up
wood, locating the same tree is difficult. Hence it is all too easy to

deviate off course.

I learn to line up on trees to my front and rear. I'm also confused about the boundaries of my area of responsibility; I veer off target and end up 300m off course. I find out when Glen roars up in the Toyota.

The work is boring, I give it that—but I am quite enjoying the solitude. The ground is now completely bare and devoid of any interest, save for the odd stunted tree. I amuse myself by jumping on ant's nests, watching their panicked helter-skelter scrabble, and roaring around on the bike. I knock off for the day when I feel my sun-clock is low enough in the sky to warrant it. The best part of the day is racing the setting sun back to the homestead before dusk. I'm loving it.

I had to be careful not to get lost. On a sojourn during shearing, I recalled Bronwyn had given me a guide to the paddocks, and after going miles or so through umpteen gates: "leave that one closed..."—"no, that one stays open," she announced we had arrived in the "middle paddock"—*but it still looked just like every other to me.* So, when I make my way back on my own, I realise I am unsure of the way. As far as I am concerned, getting lost and overnighting in the paddock is not a worry, but looking incompetent in front of Glen is.

I deal with this by skirting around the edges of paddocks, keeping to fences so I can retrace my footsteps should I get lost. Just when I am worried, I recognise one of the padlocks on a gate, and know I am on track. I am soon zooming the final three miles through familiar territory and arrive back at my cottage at dusk.

As a matter of routine, I kick off my shoes in the kitchen and sit in front of the TV. I still only get two channels in black and white—PRIME which runs endless "adverts for country folk" and Nine. How many weeks to go?

CHAPTER 8 THE CENTRAL
COAST OF NSW

As Walgett is close to Lightning Ridge, a well-known Opal mining town not far from the Queensland border, I decide to detour there before returning to Sydney. I want to have one more adventure "out back" or in the "regions". The scheduled Greyhound picks me up from outside the community park in Walgett, and heads 80 kilometres north up the Castlereagh Highway. I arrive in Lightning Ridge at about 8pm and check in to a motel on the main strip. The main road is a long, wide, street, with single-storey pizza shops, and a newsagent. I spot a very impressive bowling club with a nigh-perfect green out the front.

I have arranged to take an Opal tour on a minibus run by a former miner, and we wander around old mines and see the quaint residences of locals. The attraction is that anyone can claim a piece of land for about a hundred bucks–and then do whatever they choose with it. Marked steel pickets are used to mark out the plot which must be checked with the Mining Registrat to ensure it does not infringe on any existing claim.

The Ridge attracts the usual eccentrics, and out of the thousands of people actively working their claims, no one can be sure who is making any money. However, the town is reputed to have several "millionaires". People erect the strangest houses. One man has built a Spanish style castle complete with battlements and a drawbridge.

According to the guide, Lightning Ridge is one of several places in the world where Opal can be found. Most is found in Australia, and much of that in famous Coober Pedy, South Australia, where it is so hot that townspeople live underground in holes to keep out of the sun.

In the afternoon, I walk around the bars in the town to find a place to wind away the rest of the day. I opt for the bowling club but first decide to sink a schooner in the bar on the corner. I scan a copy of the *Daily Telegraph* and wait for an opportunity to be included in the conversation, but the blokes there are not particularly talkative. On the tv, Sydney rugby league club Manly is playing a city rival, Roosters from the west. Manly are renowned for being the "silver tails" from the affluent North Shore.

I adjourn to the Bowling Club, supposedly the largest such club in the Southern Hemisphere, with a floor area of 3,800 square metres, that's an acre—and a membership standing at about 3,600—that's 1 square metre each by my reckoning. There are several public bars, pokies (slot machines) and a "TAB" kiosk —Totalisation Agency Board, a government agency. There is one in every country club in Australia. Clubs in Australian towns are not like pubs or bars in the UK, or even Australian hotels; they are basically a "country club" fashioned in the style of a UK working man's club.

After a bland diet on the farm, I am looking forward to a "good feed". In the dining room, I order a Ribeye medium-rare from the menu and watch the other diners queuing at the counter for parmies and battered fish. They are a mixed bag, most over 35, but younger people turn up. Apart from small talk with the locals, there is not much going on in town tonight, and not another backpacker to be seen—so I return to the comfort of my motel room.

I arrive back in Dubbo, the halfway point to Sydney, and stand on the platform next to the train dreading the thought of an eight-hour train trip. Living out of a suitcase, and being on the road the last three months, is starting to tell. But the solution comes to me naturally—I will fly back to Sydney. A call to the local aerodrome and an airline there, confirms an empty seat on a flight leaving in twenty minutes. I jump in a taxi, and we race out of town towards the airfield. We pull up outside the terminal for Hazleton Airlines, where ten people are making the trip. The pilot is standing in short sleeves with a small crew, and we strike up a conversation. Maybe I could get an invite to the flight deck but these days in the year immediately post 9/11, things have changed.

We land briefly in the country town of Orange, to allow more passengers on, and soon we are descending into Sydney Domestic Terminal. After the heat of Walgett and Lightning Ridge, the autumnal Sydney weather is an agreeable 21 degrees.

***

I have accepted an offer to stay with my cousin, Martin, and his wife, Robin, with their young children, on the Central Coast of New South Wales. This entails a 90min train journey from Sydney to Gosford, a town on the edge of Brisbane Water. This section of coast is beautiful, a line of lagoons and in-land waterways, until quite recently lightly populated and untouched. Now it is a commuter's paradise, the overspill from Sydney, but still retains the neighbourly charm and quiet of a backwater.

They live in a weatherboard house on top of a hill of the beach town of Avoca. They have two school boys in primary school and a toddler, 18 months; she teeters around with an Elmo book.

I see all sorts of wildlife out in back; lots of bush turkeys, and the ubiquitous kookaburra—they land on the balcony fence outside the French windows when we eat. They resemble a huge kingfisher with large beak.

Martin and I catch up on events we remember from the early 1980s:

"I remember you coming in to my room as a young boy and mucking around with the bass on my stereo when I was trying to play my guitar," he says, "you were a right pain, mate."

Local Terrigal is beautiful, a fantastic family and locals' beach. There's a life saver club, next to the main road with cafes and bistros. At the beach is a natural grass amphitheatre, with a rugby pitch marked out, overlooked by a steep, prominent, hill that overlooks the sea. Walkers with dogs use the vantage point for exercise, and I've taken to running up and down.

On a Saturday, Martin and I are out with the boys, and a rugby game is on, so I seek out the membership secretary in the crowd. She invites me over to the Terrigal Trojans club bar after the game. After chilled tinnies, I arrange to train during the week. People are heading over to the pub, so I go over too. We watch a bit of Super 12 rugby, the rugby competition between provincial sides from New Zealand, South Africa and Australia. (The Crusaders from Canterbury, the South Island of NZ, play the New South Wales Waratahs in the semi-final winning 96–19 much to the Aussies' disappointment.)

At training, I arrive at the oval early, and kick around with some of the blokes in the incessant rain. We start off running at full power in to tackle bags—I'm soon knackered. These routines are broken up by the occasional lap around the pitch. It is in the longer shuttle races that I am dismayed to find my age catching up on me. I find the 17, 18- and 19-year-old wingers are leaving me for dead. I shake my head, and concede I am getting older. I walk in, soaked, looking like a dog's dinner.

***

One weekend, we drive to a coastal town called South West Rocks to run a clinic. Martin has a mate there called Chris, who runs a business in town.

South West Rocks, population: 3,000, is halfway up New South Wales between Sydney and Brisbane south of Coff's Harbour, on a section of coast called the Mid-North Coast. (Look at a climatic map of Australia, and you'll see it is located at the southern edge of the sub-tropical climate zone.) It's a popular holiday destination, only discovered in the 1970s, but largely ignored by young backpacker crowds who pass it over on the way to Byron

Bay, some four hours further north.

The town's principal attraction is Trial Bay Gaol, a brick jailhouse. It is an imposing edifice; more of a miniature castle than a jailhouse, with barred windows and slits set in white, but greying brick. When we arrive, we are out of season and the town is quiet.

We meet Chris, a barrel-chested, gregarious and talkative man, about 5' 7", and his glamorous wife, Julie. Cassie, 11, answers the door. Their house is atop a hill overlooking the Macleay River and the view from the sun deck stretches to the banks. Chris and I hit if off straight away, talking about our love of Rugby. He is a confident, enigmatic, charismatic man, and he invites me to stay in the winter.

CHAPTER 9 A GAME AT THE ROCKS

One of the things I assumed about Australia's weather, mistakenly, was that it was hot all the time, all-year round. The continent's publicity is surely to blame, of course, with editorial awash with photos of men with leather faces in big hats squinting across paddocks, men and women in skimpy costumes on the Sydney Eastern Beaches, and arid imagery of desert scenes surrounding Uluru (Ayer's Rock.) The tropics in the north have a wet and dry season—but down south in the temperate zone there are seasons to track.

We are going in to winter, and the days and nights are cooling. The days are now averaging 17 degrees or so– shooting to the occasional height of 22, and the nights are dropping to as low as 12. Now I know this is not that cold, but it must be, because I feel the need to put on a fleece jumper most days. What has happened, of course, is I have acclimatised to a warmer climate. The slightest drop in temperature or a sudden breeze has me reaching for a sweatshirt. In a Sydney winter, you can sit on the beach and get burnt. I am glad to miss the constant drizzle or gloom that typifies a Northern winter.

So, dressed now in fleece jacket, I am sitting in Chris's Toyota. It's the first calendar day of "upside-down" winter, First June. Chris will provide accommodation and food in exchange for me building a website for his business. They are away at a Chris Isaac concert in Sydney, so Martin brings me up. We spent Saturday night having pizza in the local pizzeria, followed by watching Kate Winslet—the lovely Kate Winslet(!) in *Holy Smoke* on Austar cable, in front of a wood fire: Australian homes are cool in the midsummer's heat, but decidedly cold in the nights.

I edge down the road in to the centre of town, finding my way around. At the Macleay river, I stop for a while by the jetty watching the occasional fishing boat. I notice a huge stone-chip in the windscreen over the passenger's side. Shit. I've got no idea how I've managed to do it. There'll be hell to pay when Chris and Julie get back this afternoon. Back at the house, I settle in luxury on the leather sofa and watch a bit of TV. I hear them arriving, and go upstairs and greet them.

"Good day!" Chris says in his usual, infectiously friendly, boisterous fashion.

"How you going, Steve," Julie adds.

In her hands she has their new hyper one-month old Maltese puppy who likes to play with the two cats a huge tabby, and a ginger.

"Fine," I say. "Erm–I have to come clean about the Camry. I think I've cracked the windscreen this morning."

Chris grins.

"Don't worry Kippers. It's been there for weeks."

Chris reckons Englishmen are fond of eating fish—kippers is a delicacy I don't share, but I don't mind being ribbed in this way —there's always been a healthy rivalry between the Aussies and the "Old Country".

***

Chris introduces me to the staff in the auto parts factory. Roger, aged 40—as a sign in his area testifies—has worked with Chris for seven years. He is balding, slim and rangy, and wears paddock boots with socks folded and cuffed over the top of the elastic sides. Next—Gary, aged about 65, with short red hair. He is afflicted with Agent Orange poisoning he was exposed to in a factory years before. He also has the dubious distinction of having served time in prison for armed robbery thirty years previously, when he was one of a group of men who held up a servo (petrol station.) He is happy-go-lucky, and is keen to chat.

I can't get over how friendly everyone is; on my brief forays out to shops in the Bi-Lo shopping mall, everyone stops to chat. London now seems far away. My first weeks in South West Rocks are a blur of making new acquaintances and hearing all sorts of gossip which you would expect to hear in a small town.

On Friday evening, Chris and I head over for a schooner at the pub which looks out over the beach road. Chris is the perfect host, funny, engaging, always the life and soul of the party. He is a keen sportsman and knows most of the cricketers and footie players in town. He opens the batting in First Grade, but played prop in league in his younger days. Ten years ago, he broke his back working at heights. Part of his recovery was the hours of swimming he did to strengthen his neck and shoulders, and when he, Cassie and I swim, he battles through surf with ease. I disguise my lack of swimming style by splashing Cassie in the shallows.

In the early 1980s, he coached young players, and as his brother plays front row for the South West Rocks Jailers, he will try to get me a game. During my second week, his brother comes in to the factory to introduce himself. I take an instant liking to him. A year younger than me, about 6 foot, well-built and slightly chubby, he is like me, blond, with a mischievous grin and a smiling, outgoing, talkative personality.

"Training is Mondays, Steve. See you there."

***

The Football World Cup is on, and Australia has taken an interest in the tournament. It is not well known that Australia's biggest participation sport is soccer as the television mainly shows Rugby League and Aussie Rules. I catch a game on Chris's bar TV through a snow-storm reception.

We've been invited to Roger's house the night of the England–Argentina match. He lives with his wife in a beautifully made-over, landscaped house out in the bush on the edge of town. Outside, a pool area with a patio in the Spanish style with pillars supporting a roofed bar-b-que area. It could be a holiday villa belonging to an English couple on the Costa del Sol. Music pipes from one of the bedrooms overlooking the pool.

I meet a few locals, one of whom is a beautician, a flirty blonde woman in her early thirties, and her friends. The England game comes on. There's Aussies supporting the "old country". Roger's son is a trainee builder with bright bleached spiky hair, and he is cheering on the "poms".

By Sunday, it is warmish, so I decide to chuck on my Speedos and jump in the pool for a swim. I announce this to Cassie, and her face flickers in a look of amusement. She follows me outside and watches me lower myself in. I realise my mistake straight away. It may be warm currently, and this may be Australia; but it's bloody cold. Cassie laughs, and calls Julie over, then reaches for the dangling thermometer.

"It's 12 degrees, Mum," she cries gleefully.

Chris joins me in training at the Oval the next night, and I am introduced to the coach. Whilst we wait for the players, Chris and I warm up—he is going to join in too. He puts up high balls, and even under the helpful illumination of the spotlights, I miss several. Safety under the high ball is not my forte, although I am looking forward to turning on the afterburners. It's been a while though.

In 2000, I was a debutante winger for the Luxembourg rugby club. The team was made up of English, Welsh, Scots, Australians and New Zealander players—plus a native-born Luxembourger who we called "Token". The club provided a team to play in World Cup Qualifiers, even if we never won against Sweden or even Germany. I was back playing the game in my late twenties—probably over the hill.

I was itching to go in one match we played. We were playing a team in the Belgian league. Our Number Ten gathered the ball, and we attacked from inside our half. He chose to run, and my outside centre offloaded to me with 30 metres to go. It was a straightforward race to the try line. I remember now how I pinned my ears back, and turned on the afterburners.

As I reached the tryline, I sensed the defending full-back closing in to tackle. I launched myself for the line with arms outstretched—not sure whether I would make it there. I remember the encouraging cheer from the crowd, and when I walked back to the halfway line, the way my coach caught my eye.

I am sore in the morning, after training, so book an appointment with the local chiropractor who lives in a small house around the corner from Chris. He is a recent mover to the town. I list my injuries and frailties, while he sympathetically listens. There was whiplash from sport where I was treated by a wacky (and expensive) chiropractor in Holborn. This chiro examines me and adds that one of my shoulders is higher than the other. Indeed it is: that's a 1987 left clavicle green-stick fracture whilst cycling to school.

Matchday is bright and cheerful, a beautiful winter's day. As we are early, the coach pencils me in at Number 11, my preferred wing slot. I do a few warm-up laps around the pitch and sit in the sun on the touchline and watch the under 17s play their game.

The match is uneventful, and I see very little ball. Our Number Ten kicks the ball high towards the opposition. I am the first to arrive, but the opposing winger has time to collect. Next, when I gather in my own 22, rather than kick, I decide to run it out. Not so good—I get tackled, and dutifully cough up the ball. Their full-back puts the ball down for a try. I can't believe my stupidity. When we go in to half-time behind, I am not surprised to be subbed.

The highlight of the second half is beautiful running from a young aboriginal player who executes fantastic chip and chases, much to the crowd's delight. A player from the opposing team goes off with a split head, with blood pouring from his forehead. We win the game, no thanks to me. Chris has seen my error, so I sheepishly walk over to him.

"Never mind Kippers," he says.

During the week, Chris has work in Armidale and Tamworth,

located on the New England plateau, inland. The plateau is renowned for hot, dry summers, and cold, bitter, winters. Further west, it drops off to the New South Wales North West Slopes and then Riverina both ideal for farming. He has invited me along, and I am more than happy to join him for the ride and change of scenery. I pack a fleece. Chris knocks on my door at about 5am and we creep in to the garage. It is a chilly four degrees, and so we have the AC on to de-mist the windows. We take the Pacific Highway north. The sun comes up to warm our faces as we are on the highway towards Armidale. The Toyota is comfortable over the distance: Chris has the cruise-control on and has his snakeskin-booted legs crossed and relaxed in front of him.

Armidale is nestled at 1000m, and Chris parks up in a residential road minutes from the town centre. I leave him to get on with his business and walk in to the centre past an old Anglican church with graveyard—old by colonial standards anyhow. Armidale is also a college town for the University of New England and has a student population.

It is now very fresh, about seven degrees, and townspeople are dressed for the climate, in scarves and gloves. Leaves cover the streets and the trees are bare. The architecture in places is 19th century, a sort of American New England feel. I look around the cafes and bookshops and gentleman outfitters—at the epic displays of Akubras, Driz-a-Bones and RM Williams boots, and look at prices—on parity with Sydney.

Soon we are on our way to Tamworth. It's a much bigger town, known for Australia's sporting horse industry and Country Music Festival. Whilst Chris nips in to businesses, I sit at a café in the sub-tropical sun and eat an enormous "Works Burger"—a hamburger with all the "works" which here, include beetroot for local palates.

***

The World Cup England–Brazil Quarter Final match is on Friday. Chris and I head to the club and watch the first half and am pleased to see England take the lead. This could be England's year, as if we can dispatch Brazil, surely we can beat anyone in the Final. In the second half, with Brazil going ahead 2–1, It is clear what is required: England must score to take the game in to extra time, but I cannot bear to watch and turn away.

"Turning your back on your team Kippers!" crows Chris, taking a sip of Extra Dry from his stubbie.

England lose.

I get to travel with Chris further afield once more, this time to Lismore, not far from Byron Bay. We have morning tea in a milk bar set in the American 1950s, with signs and menus, and a display of Lamington cakes. Lamington is a kind of Australian sponge cake with coconut flakes.

The town itself has a hippy vibe and influence, as befits a centre near Byron Bay, and the streets are full of girls walking around with jaunty hip bones exposed, with their ruler-straight flat and toned stomachs pressed against low-slung hipsters, hair in braids. I browse the fishing and gun shops. On the way back south, we are cut up by an errant driver, and Chris curses at the driver.

"Couldn't drive a tack up a bull's arse with a frying pan!"

There is more sport to come in this sports-mad country though. The train takes me down to Sydney the last Friday of June, as I have tickets for the Australia–France Second Test, again at Stadium Australia. It is colder south, and the evening is bitterly cold. I stand next to Ben Tune, the Australian winger who has been out injured, and listen to his pre-match broadcast. He signs a mini-rugby ball I have bought for my cousin's children.

I stand self-consciously for the National anthems wearing an Australian scarf to ward against the wind, (even though I don't know the words.) I sit on my plastic seat in the stand fortified by hot chips (french fries) and shiver in to my Driz-a-Bone.

CHAPTER 10 TROPICAL TRIP

I n the middle of winter, I decide to get away for a couple of weeks from the cold New South Wales nights, and head up to northern Queensland for a tropical break of sight-seeing, beaches and scuba diving. I also plan a 4x4 safari further south on Fraser Island, the world's largest sand island. On the way up there, I plan to drop in on more relatives.

My cousin, Rachael, lives not far from South West Rocks in Coff's Harbour, so I spend the week with Julie and Chris at South West Rocks, making adjustments to the website as we will launch at the weekend.

The Great Britain and Ireland Rugby League touring side will play Friday night. Chris has put a bet on both ways. He has a few blokes over to watch it, and in his lounge room, amongst catcalls and laughter—even Julie is smirking—I sink lower and lower in my chair as GB are put to the sword. Chris turns to me:

"Is it your turn to bat, yet, Kippers?" he crows.

However, on Saturday, he is not so smug, when in the opening round of the Tri-Nations in Christchurch, New Zealand beat Australia 12–6 in the wind and wet.

"There you go, Chris," I laugh.

Rachael arrives in an old grey Mazda to pick me up. I haven't seen her since I was a teenager in London when she regaled us with her life in Sydney and tales of film-extra work. She started out on *Home and Away*. She has a library of out-takes on video, and in them, variously: she is a nurse, a receptionist, and a police officer. Perhaps her finest hour was playing a journalist in *Muriel's Wedding*, one of Australia's most successful film export comedies from the mid-1990s starring Toni Collette (*Sixth Sense*.) She also appeared in a Fosters advert and played a stewardess in the well-known 1990s "The spaceships have landed" advert for the Ansett airline.

***

Standing around on film sets seems to run in the family. When I was at university in London, a friend, Julian, had been telling us about his work in his latest film, *First Knight*, with Richard Gere, Sean Connery and Ben Cross (*Chariots of Fire.*)

A lot of blokes I knew in my infantry company got work over the years. One with an equity card got a role in the 1989 *Batman* movie; a speaking part as a croupier. He also had a close-up shot in *Full Metal Jacket*, firing an anti-tank missile—and had worked as an archer in *Henry V*. Blokes had played Nazis in *Indiana Jones and the Last Crusade*, and Jim Bayliss, who was in my training platoon, appeared in *A Breed of Heroes* in the mid-1990s. There's a scene where the camera tracks into a noisy barrack room and he's doing pull-ups on a wooden beam, bare-chested. And, Dave, back in London, was already filming in the next *Harry Potter*.

I rang up a friend who was out of work, and we turned up at Pinewood. We met Julian in the Production office, where a casting assistant sizes us up.

"Yup, they're in," she says.

He took us over to Wardrobe to try on armour for size, then Hair and Make-up: having foundation applied to our faces. We were ready to play the "Marauders"—the "Bad Guys", led by Malagant, played by the old stalwart Ben Cross.

On the outdoor lot, a massive fibreglass golden castle, representing Camelot, had been built, held up by scaffolding. In one scene, Malagant attacks Camelot Castle interrupting a trial where Sean Connery (King Arthur) challenges Richard Gere (Sir Lancelot.) His knights race on horseback into the courtyard through the archway, his foot soldiers surrounding the Royal Guards. Malagant makes a speech to the people of Camelot, and King Arthur is about to kneel before him when he springs up and shouts for his court to "fight and never surrender". The effects guys have arranged for him to be struck in the chest by a volley of arrows which is the signal for us to clash with swords.

For the last day of the shoot, I played the part of a villager (we can call them "the good guys".) There was a close-up scheduled with Ben Cross and Richard Gere, requiring stuntmen and extras fighting in the background. Julian had been discussing the shot with Jerry Zucker's assistant and asked him whether he could use a "few more blokes" so he plucked me from a cast of tens.

I found a sword in the props trolley, and we rehearsed a sequence for the takes, sidling up and down in front of the cameras, being careful not to knock over the principals. I saw the movie in an upstate New York multiplex the next year, working on a summer camp, and was thrilled to see myself on a balcony holding a burning torch, even if they were only brief cuts.

***

Rachael and I, and her 18-month old daughter, Beatrice, spend a few days pottering around Coff's Harbour. Rachael drives me up in to the mountains, past banana plantations and orchids to a scenic viewpoint. We visit the Big Banana, a giant fibreglass spectacle for tourists.

I leave at about 3am on a freezing cold winter's night in the last week of July, and traipse with my rucksack down to the station where I stand in the warmth of the waiting room. The train bound north for Brisbane is on time, and I settle in to my seat. On arrival in Brisbane, I'll fly north to the tropical town of Townsville. I fall asleep on the flight. Halfway, I wake up, confused. I walk to the back of the plane to say "Hi" to the crew. I go back to my seat, and flop into it, only to find I've got the wrong one.

"G'Day!" a woman says, in surprise.

"How you going?" I reply.

We yack most of the way. It turns out she is flying back home from a business trip running an import/export company. She grew up on a rural property in Queensland. On touchdown, I am pleased to see the tropical winter sun glaring in through the windows, and we step off to find it's a more agreeable 25 degrees.

Townsville, located not far from Cairns, is home to a large proportion of Australia's military forces and is a kind of drop-off point for the trip to Magnetic Island. It's a tranquil attractive place, eight miles off the mainland, and I plan to head over there.

The town itself is not particularly appealing, more of a service town, not a destination of choice. I get organised in a room I share with a group of French travellers. The hostel is big and airy, but rather uninspiring. I find the TV room and find it occupied by a girl stretched out asleep on one of several sofas facing the TV set. I flick through the channels and find a game on. The girl stirs,wakes up, and watches through drowsy, half-closed eyes.

Sally calls me, who having finished her job further south at Rockhampton, has been working her way up the Queensland coast via Airlie Beach. She's arriving here tonight, so we arrange to catch up.

"Steve. Over here," she calls when she sees me.

She is wearing her trademark floral sarong. She looks healthy and well. She looks pleased to see me and gives me a hug. She is tanned from station work and has plenty of stories to tell. We go off and sink pints of Guinness in the Irish bar, swapping stories. The travails of work feature—Sally's boss was constantly forgetting supplies from town, which meant, unlike me, they were going in to town practically every day. Her boss was a nice enough man, and she cooked for him most days. She shows me photographs including one of her on horseback with her cattle, which she grew quite attached to.

"Do you know," she says, "my boss said to me one day; 'Sally, I've known you two weeks, and I haven't had as much as one kiss from you'."

The trials and tribulations of a cowgirl working on a cattle station.

The next day, we say goodbye, as she shoulders her backpack, and heads off up north towards Cairns and a job packing bananas on a fruit farm near there. I board the ferry to Magnetic

Island. After a 30-minute ride, we disembark at a long jetty at Picnic Bay.

The bay is an idyllic spot in the Caribbean mould; unspoiled and sleepy looking. Groups of backpackers relax in walled gardens waiting for lifts or friends. A sandy, and for now, deserted beach is metres away. There is a token collection of bars and shops here, with people grazing—and gazing—into space.

There's a place hiring out Mini Mokes and I grab one. It doesn't take a minute to find the coast road. I power out of Picnic Bay, around a tiny roundabout, and head north-east on the coastal road out towards Horseshoe Bay.

I find Coconuts in Nelly Bay. It lies directly on the beach, comprising a beach bar and kitchen, scuba operation, and a little village of cabins arranged precariously along a deep gorge. A wooden catwalk provides access to the rooms. It looks like an Ewok village. My cabin is cramped and dirty, with four beds—mattresses covered in sand, but no one seems to mind as the atmosphere is very relaxed and party-on.

Costed in to my room fee is three pitchers of cocktail—heavily diluted—plus a meal from the kitchen. At the bar, I get talking to three teenaged backpackers, who tell me about their skydiving experiences over Mission Beach. I offer them a lift to the local shops, and they jump in gratefully. One of them asks me:

"Are you English?" I reply in the affirmative.

"Well–you've got an Australian accent."

It looks as if months of staying on the station, on the Central Coast and at South West Rocks has had an effect on my accent; my vowels are longer, I speak slower, and I am losing my accent.

Back at Coconuts, I sit at one of the bar tables and relax, opening a tatty copy of *Men Of Men* by Wilbur Smith, which I found in the TV room. A slim girl with straight long legs, and wavy blonde hair comes up to me.

"Are you Dave?" I think she asks.

At least I think that's what she said.

"No–I'm Steve," I reply, squinting upwards.

"No–do you deeve?" she asks again.

Then I realise—she's Irish. And she's asking me if I *dive.*

"Yes I do!" I reply.

"Good. I need a buddy to dive with now. I want to do a shore dive. Do you want to come?"

"OK," I say.

"I'm Carrie."

We head over to the PADI dive shop and don wetsuits, tanks, BCDs, and pick up masks, fins and snorkels. One of the supervisors tells us where we can go to find interesting water. I tell Carrie that I have not dived for a bit, and therefore need to wing it. So giggling, we head around the corner, where we go through buddy checks. We wade out in to the sea and are soon swimming through the shallows underwater.

I'm impressed with Carrie's experience, less so with her sense of direction, so I point at my compass and indicate the way. When we surface, I suggest we go for a drive and lunch in Horseshoe Bay. She agrees. With an appetite, we have a slap-up meal of steak and chips in a beachfront bar, washed down with schooners of Castlemaine.

It is getting dark, and we sit next to backpackers on a table overlooking the beach and watch the sun go down on the sea, casting changing bands of colour. The moon comes up, poking its head over the sea horizon, and we watch its ascension. It is of dinner-plate proportions, and predictably casts a path all the way down to the beach. There are gasps of delight as people turn around. A group of people walk out in to the water for a night dive, and their silhouettes descend in to the black, safety lights just visible.

***

I awake to hear noise coming from outside the hut, presumably coming from the space between each. I can hear a couple in the grass, right outside the eaves, and every sound filters through as if they are lying right next to me. A breeze directs me to a meshed ventilation strip above my head. The couple talk, and whisper for ages, with the occasional giggle, but I am not awake for long and I drift back to sleep.

I am awoken again by a gasp, and a groan. I hear a murmur —then the unmistakable sound of a girl's orgasm. Someone in the hut next door bangs on the walls of their hut. "Good luck to them" is my attitude. I turn over sleepily.

My eyes open when the Danish girl above climbs out of bed and stands in front of me getting dressed. She is nude. People talk amongst themselves: an athletic girl from Wales hides her blushes. She kept a fair bit of the camp awake last night.

CHAPTER 11 OPEN WATER

B ack at Picnic Bay at the jetty, a large cruise ferry is waiting which is going to take us out to the Great Barrier Reef. The trip to the outer reef is about two hours, and whilst we cruise, the crew put on instructional videos, and organise divers and snorkelers. There's a buffet lunch of sandwiches, cake, fruit and juice. The day is hot, and the sky is blue; perfect conditions —the sea state is calm, and the visibility good.

As we approach the Reef, the only clue is the water darkening in the distance—the unseen underwater reef formations—and there are more birds around. We stop, and the snorkelers duck-foot down ladders to the water's edge. It's quite a sight to see so many people face-down in the water. Meanwhile we struggle in to our gear. I zip up my trousers and catch my thigh, which leaves a nasty bruise. My dive buddy is an experienced PADI divemaster from London, with hundreds of dives under his belt, and he stands some way off, with an amused look on his face.

A waiting dinghy with outboard takes us out. Everyone has been so busy with their gear and immersed in their own private thoughts, the coxswain looks around our faces with surprise.

"Why is everyone so miserable?" he asks, hoping to get a reaction.

When we get over to the dive site, we sink in to the sea, and on the descend signal, inch hand over hand down the line there to a depth of about 13 metres. Initially, the water is full of bubbles from everyone's exhausts, and it is difficult to see, but soon it clears up and we can see the marine life.

My buddy stays away from the rabble, and I stick with him, enjoying the water free from bubbles or kicked-up silt. He keeps his arms by his side, so he maintains a streamlined shape. The wildlife is amazing, and we swim over mountains of coral. One moment we have metres of water between us and the sea bed, and next, we have to pick our way carefully to avoid disturbing it. The allotted time goes by in no time, and soon we get the signal to surface.

"How was that?" asks one of the instructors, back on boat.

"A bit short," grumbles a girl.

When we return to the cruise boat, we find lunch is being served, and we join the back of a large queue of chattering snorkellers waiting to be served. No sooner do we eat a few mouthfuls, it is time to get geared up for our second dive.

"Get on the bus, get off the bus", an expression from my military days, rings in my head.

The second dive is barely ten metres, but we sit on the bottom and feed fish, which is a real treat, as huge species swim close to us. Back on the boat, we wrestle out of our wetsuits, all elbows and arms.

Coconuts is hosting a "Full Moon Party", and a band arrives, together with locals from Townsville and all over Mag. The Australia-South Africa Tri-Nations *rah-rah* game being played in Brisbane is shown live on the bar TV. I get talking to some blokes from Townsville, one is an ex British Army Sergeant who has migrated to Australia and got a job as a contractor with the Australian Defence Force servicing helicopters. He can barely believe his luck. A girl from my room, from Norway, I think, who lost her wallet the night before, walks around the drinkers, sitting on blokes' laps, kissing them, before moving on to someone else. Everyone is in party mood.

***

I head back south down the Queensland coast on the Greyhound, and pass through the popular resort of Airlie Beach, and head on to Hervey Bay, which is famous for whale-watching this time of year. In the morning, we pass through Childers, the scene of the 2000 hostel fire which claimed 13 lives, set in rolling *Lord of The Rings* verdant countryside: there is something of the UK South Downs.

We are met at Harvey Bay bus station by a pod of minibuses, all advertising 4x4 trips to nearby Fraser Island, 70 miles long. It's the largest sand island in the world, with miles of dunes to get lost in.

In for a penny, in for a pound. I get on a bus driven by a friendly looking man in his fifties.

We are ushered in to the bar where we receive a safety briefing from Adrian, a funny and exuberant local. Driving 4x4s on Fraser Island can be a dangerous business. Every year, hundreds of tourists manage to roll their vehicles in the soft sand or collide with other vehicles on the highway.

We get tips on driving in low range through sand dunes and points are reinforced with video clips and pictures. When he gets to the pictures of overturned vehicles and mentions fatalities, some of the backpackers look worried, and exchange looks of concern.

"This bloke was driving along the beach in cruise mode, and completely forgot about the deep-water channels you get every so often. There's a particularly wide one here."

He indicates a blue line on the map.

"He thought he would re-enact the scene in *Thelma and Louise* and flew across it at 80 or 100 kilometres per hour. The 'Cruiser was a right off and a loose piece of gear took someone's head off. Be careful out there."

A few backpackers are exchanging comments. One bloke is caught talking. Adrian interjects:

"Mate, can you listen to what I am saying here? You're going to look a bit dumb if you stuff up."

The backpacker, a boy aged about 21, looks up, with a startled expression on his face, which then soon turns to annoyance.

"Don't talk to me like that. Yeah!"—Adrian looks annoyed, and looks at him condescendingly—"I mean, who looks the dick now? So, you can't just drive like it's Baywatch out there, OK? Stay out of the water."

There's one more point about the 4x4s. Any saltwater getting into the chassis is bad news: any corrosion found in the bottom of our vehicles will lose us our deposits.

He also talks to us about how we must deal with dingos. They've received a bad press over the years. There have been a series of fatal attacks. (The most infamous case is the 1980 case of a baby that was taken from a campsite that made headlines all over the world.) The message is clear—do not feed them, and do not leave food lying around.

We are divided in to two groups, and allocated a Toyota Land Cruiser, equipped with a large roof-rack for camp gear. Part of the group are allocated to food-shopping duties and head to Woolworths to buy food for the ten of us with a budget and shopping list.

On the way back, we discover the other group fuming. Their shoppers went out and blew their budget.

"Look at this useless junk we have to eat," complains one girl.

It's an early start at the vehicles. We are given final reminders by the staff. One reaches in to a glove compartment and fishes out a small plastic box.

"Here's the first aid kit. It's got plenty of bandages in it. The only reason behind this is if one of the girls cuts her finger cooking, dinner will still be on the table in time. OK?"

He grins and pretends to ignore the raised eyebrows from the girls. We get in, and I swing in to the driver's seat, as I have been assigned driving duties.

We arrive at the ferry terminal where I back the Cruiser on to the ferry. Everyone is told to get out whilst I do it, and board by the passenger gangplank. With hundreds of eyes on me, I reverse carefully up the ramp, to a spot indicated by a loadmaster.

On disembarking, we take our place in a long line of 4x4s heading down the sand road to the main central station.

We stop at a lake, a small and largely untouched beauty area, where we swim and sunbake for about an hour. The lake is a deep aquamarine, surrounded by pine trees. We've been told the sand has metal-cleaning properties, so a few backpackers take their watches off and give it a go. We play impromptu soccer, barefoot on the lakeside and kick up sand.

Finally, we get to 75-mile beach. Scores of vehicles approach us in the opposite direction, and we keep over to the left. We find a good campsite up the beach in a sheltered spot, near the tree line. Whilst part of the group put up the tents, others set up the camp kitchen. I work on the fire. Two rangers turn up and inspect our progress and stand around, with probably not much to do.

"Youse guys going alright?" one says.

The other group arrives and sets up, and they seem keen to make up for being slower; they have a fire crackling away in no time. We perch by the fire, enjoying backpackers' spaghetti bolognaise. Someone plays his torch around and exclaims. He has picked out a dingo standing nearby in trees. Its eyes flash in the torchlight, then it flees. We spot more pacing in the shadows, but they retreat as soon as they are picked out by our wandering beams. By midnight, most of the group are comfortably inebriated and we collect on the beach, watching the surf roll in and stroke the shore.

Rubbing the sleep out of our eyes, we just about make it away in time, as we need to get to the north of the island before the tide comes in. There's a particularly nasty sand field. The Land Cruiser bogs in, and remembering the advice, we get out, lightening the load. The driver engages first gear, dumps the clutch, and with us all pushing hard, shifts it. Whipping through the gear changes, he "revs the tits" (as the locals say) off the engine and powers up the dune.

On foot, at the top of the cliff, we look out in to the ocean crashing against the rocks below, before hitting the beach to leeward. We can see schools of dolphins swimming below, flitting around, playing in the rips and tides of the water. We also see the occasional menacing shark.

Picture the scene. As we are standing on the beach after our exertions, talking amongst ourselves, we hear a huge roar—it is absolutely deafening. We look up. Two fast jets, belonging to the

Royal Australian Air Force, come screaming low level over the cliff, so low we feel they are actually about to crash; they tear off down 75-mile beach.

"****ing hell!" someone cries.

"Did you see that?" says someone else.

Pretty close, I think we can all agree.

Once the tide goes out, we negotiate the headland, and pick a site to camp. It is set in flat grassland, 100 metres from the beach protected by onshore breezes. As dark falls, I chop up the firewood, and a steak chef back home in the US takes over the grilling and cooks the meat to everyone's satisfaction.

After more story swapping, people go to bed one by one, but a hard core manage to get to 4am.

At breakfast, people are seedy: a breeze swirls through the camp, and a dingo arrives and watches us. We head inland to visit Lake Wabby, reached by a long winding forest track which opens out in a moonscape of rolling dunes. Feeling like characters from *Lawrence of Arabia*, we trek across desert for half an hour before emerging by a lakeside oasis.

Tired and elated, we head back on the ferry to Hervey Bay, where everyone is subdued after the excitement of the last days.

***

I head back to Brisbane, a half a day's drive south. Brisbane is Australia's third-biggest city after Sydney and Melbourne and enjoys a warm and muggy climate. Sandwiched between the ritzy Sunshine and Gold Coasts, it is currently Australia's fastest-growing city. I am picked up from the bus station by a friend of Chris who has invited me to stay with him.

He emigrated from South Africa in the 1970s, in the days when a visitor could go into an immigration office and fill in a few forms. He is an actor and runs a successful Karaoke on the side, and lives not far from the Gabba, the state football stadium, where the British and Irish Lions beat Australia on their tour in

2001.

That night, he is booked in to a hotel garden, and I help him shift his equipment. We arrive at the bar with amplifiers, mikes, TVs, consoles, speakers and set up. After a beer, I join in, singing along to Britney Spears—girls in low-slung hipster jeans, plastic belts and jewels in their belly buttons join in. I even muster a few classic numbers soaring up to the high tenor notes, I used to get to easily, just about getting there.

He drops me off at the Roma Street Terminal in the morning, and I get the night bus south to Sydney where I hope to pick up more work.

CHAPTER 12 BONDI – AND
ON THE ROAD AGAIN

I 've found a little job in North Sydney, in an office block on the Pacific Highway, up the hill from the North Shore line train station. My brief is to handle sales for an insurance salesman, an ex-football player in the 1960s and 1970s. He had the dubious honour of being Ken Irvine's wingman, and whilst he didn't enjoy the same international success of Ken, nonetheless played one game for New South Wales in 1965. (As for the job: I have no idea what I am doing, so thank God for the internet.)

I'm living on Bondi beach, that English hot spot. The first day of September coincides with spring arriving in Sydney, and the mornings are sunny and warm. I am staying at Indy's on Hall Street, and every morning, I walk to the beach. I love these early mornings; the sun has been up for some time, and it is mild.

I join the throng of commuters on the North Shore line and stand on the left-hand side as the train emerges from underground and out on to the Harbour Bridge. The view is a treat for any jaded worker. To ring the changes, I get the ferry to North Sydney from Circular Quay; and walk from the quay up a narrow, cobbled street. Feels a smidge like London.

Bondi life is good. I'm sharing—this week—a room with three other Londoners, all blokes. They talk in loud, boisterous, cockney tones. One addresses everyone as "Geezer". He has an eye for the ladies and can be found most nights in the TV room with his arms around a girl, often a different one each time. He's also a part-time model.

There are constant gaggles of people coming and going in the hostel, but there are also long-stay cliches. Most evenings, we go over to Coyote's, a restaurant with a bar at the back to take advantage of happy hours. The same music is on loop every night, and with a bit of experience, it is possible to tell the time by what song is up next. One saving grace—at the same time every night, the two English barmaids get up, set the bar on fire, and perform a choreographed dance routine, impressive every time you see it.

"We made it up at lunch," one says.

I am fond of a Welsh girl who works at several jobs and is consequently often not at the hostel when I am. On some weeknights, she stays up late and watches the chess club play, which suits me. She is 25, blonde, and very down to earth. She is intelligent, but quiet, which I find difficult, as we don't have much to talk about. She often sits with a boyish 20-year old redhead who is very immature, but friendly to her, like a brother. Most nights, at about 2am in the early hours, she and he go through a little pantomime, which involves him getting drunk and propositioning her.

One night, they come in together. He runs his head under the sink tap and collapses in a coma on the kitchen table bench, so she detaches from him, and walks around the kitchen, delving in to everyone's food box. People snigger.

"That's what happens when the two quietest people in the hostel get drunk," someone says.

She comes and sits on the table in front of me, helping herself to my Big Mac meal, picking out the onions and salad from my burger, leaning her head back, and dropping the food in to her mouth.

One day, I am sitting on my bed organising myself when a girl comes in, laden with a rucksack and a day bag, talking.

"This looks good! A room full of blokes." We exchange glances, and regard her as she chatters away to us. She drops her bag on the floor and sorts through its contents.

I get up, and she remarks:

"That's muscly legs you've got there. Are you a cyclist?"

"Running," I reply.

Where's this going?

"OK," she says.

It turns out she is a doctor. After she gets herself organised, we go for a coffee in Speedos on the North side of Bondi beach. I join her, and nurses from Essex for drinks at the Beach Road Hotel. We have a dance and head down to the beach, giggling. We run towards the water's edge before finally, sitting on the sand. The romantic moment is ruined by her realisation that on the run down, she has lost a trainer. We comb the beach and find it, before going to sit by the water's edge. She nestles her head in my shoulder, and we look out to the surf.

***

"Look what I found at Kempsey," announces Chris, as we step through the door connecting the garage to the house.

"Now who would that be?" asks Julie, looking up from the kitchen worktop. "Hello Steve. How you going?"

"Good Julie," I reply.

I've come up to South West Rocks to escape Bondi for a bit. Last week, the AFL season concluded as the Collingwood Magpies lost to the Brisbane Lions, who won the comp for the second consecutive time. Bondi was packed, and the Beach hotel was printing money as the spring crowds enjoyed the sunshine and increasing temperatures. It was like the circus had come to town. The New Zealand Warriors are playing the Sydney Roosters in a NRL Grand Final. The kiwis are going mad, as it is the first time a kiwi side has reached a Grand Final. It's going to be quite a weekend.

On Saturday night, we are heading out. I creep across the floor of the garage to the spare shower, past Chris's Harley Davidson. I step over the front wheel, slip, and bang my head on a shelf jutting out. It hurts like hell, and I dance around in front of the parked Camry, clutching my forehead. Taking my hand away, I spy a fair bit of fresh claret. I stagger over to the garage door, trying not to drip blood on the floor. I call out to Cassie, who is watching TV.

"Cassie!"

She comes running over, takes one look at my head, bursts in to tears, and turns away to go downstairs.

"Get your Dad!" I cry out at her retreating form.

He inspects the wound.

"It's OK, Steve, you don't need stitches."

After getting showered and changed, I am feeling better, if sore. Julie is standing by the worktop.

"You've given yourself quite a bump there, Steve," she says.

The Grand Final is chiefly memorable for a spate of injuries that see Campion, one of the NRL's hard men, sustain a head injury for the second week running. The boys all laugh at the sight of claret spilling down his face.

"There you go Kippers," laughs Chris, looking in my direction. "How's that for a bit of Cab Sav!"

Despite a hard fight from Stacey Jones and the Warriors, the Roosters win 30–8 in a good game, their first silverware since 1975. The win also returned the trophy to Sydney for the first time since Manly took the 1996 premiership.

***

To get back on the road, I have booked a seat on the train going to Adelaide, the state capital of South Australia, but first, I have to finish work that comes my way.

Getting cash in hand jobs is relatively easy; able-bodied males wanting labouring work wait by the phone in the hostel in the mornings, and tradesmen call in, or come by. I get work doing house refurbishment by an owner-operator partnership of two South African brothers who are chasing the Sydney house price boom. One of the rather eccentric brothers takes me to Randwick to a unit on the first floor in an imposing block, where he introduces me to his older brother, who is decorating the lounge room.

In the bathroom, he shows me how to tile. He describes their prospects, and pulls out a suburb listing from his back pocket showing me the price he thinks he can get for this reno.

"Steve–the median unit price for Randwick is 600k," he says running his sticky finger along an Excel spreadsheet.

Realising he has distracted himself, he then does "another one" followed by "one more" for good measure.

"Steve, you'll get it, I promise you."

He does another one. I watch politely, but this time feigning interest, I pass him the tools. An hour later, he is still busy tiling, whilst chatting. Let me tell you: at standard hourly rates, it's the easiest "labouring" money I've earnt. To cap it all, a bunch of real estate agents turn up and amble through the reno, hands in pockets, clearly not listening to the pitch he has prepared. He grumbles they don't want to hear his personalised story and sulks for a bit.

The Great Southern Railway's Indian Pacific train leaves from Sydney Central twice a week, on Thursdays and Mondays. It makes stops out in rural New South Wales at Broken Hill, Adelaide, South Australia, the mining town of Kalgoorlie, arriving in Perth after three nights and around 2,500 miles. There's a backpacker special offer; for 350 dollars, we have six months unlimited travel on Southern Railways between Perth, Alice, Adelaide and Sydney. It is a major trip, and I am quite excited about the prospect of seeing the desert plains of the Nullarbor and the expanse of the West. I plan to break my trip in Adelaide, and in Kalgoorlie, I will sound out the opportunities for well-paid mining and drilling work in the "wild west".

Days before I am due to leave to head west for South Australia, a bomb detonates in Bali, killing 183 people, Australians amongst them. It's the first time in living memory Australians have suffered an attack of that magnitude, and the story runs for weeks. Bali is one of the most popular holiday destinations; it is cheaper to fly there from Perth than to Sydney, but my mode of transport will be the train.

On a Thursday, I walk down the platform, looking for my seat. The train is at least 20 carriages long, half a mile in length, and people have driven their cars on to take across the continent.

These people travel on the train because they want to and can afford to, when it is cheaper—and quicker—to fly between the state capitals. In Gold Kangaroo service, patrons enjoy ensuites to themselves, and a plush dining room, with flash meals served by waiters. In Red Kangaroo—a polite way of saying economy class—service, at the back of the train, I find a lounge car, and a buffet car. The air-conditioning in the lounge car is turned up a notch to deter backpackers from sleeping in there and the senior conductor wakes you up on his hourly rounds should you try.

So, in this modicum of comfort, I settle myself for a day's journey to Broken Hill and Adelaide. About 24 hours after leaving Sydney, the train crosses New South Wales and we arrive in Broken Hill, so close to the South Australia border it is on their time—Central time—half an hour behind. The scenery outside the train is barren and bleak; featureless desert.

Broken Hill might be an oasis of sorts in this desert, a collection of streets arranged in a grid system. It's larger than expected. We have a couple of hours to get off the train and explore. I've been talking to one of the girls in my carriage called Rebecca, who like me, has been jackerooing in New South Wales, and is also going on to Adelaide. She is excited, as she likes Brett, one of the stewards in the buffet car who is ex-Australian Navy, and served in Iraq in the early 90s. She was up all night talking to him. As he gets off shift in Adelaide himself where he lives, he has invited her for a drink. She is well informed but with a tendency to make sure she can beat you in everything she does: another "Two-shit Tyler", but good company.

She and I walk through the streets of Broken Hill and get a coffee at a corner cafe. We get back on the train as they sound the whistle, and we cross in to South Australia, the hottest, driest state: two-thirds covered by desert. It is infamous for housing Woomera, the prison for illegal arrivals in Australia.

We chug through desert all morning, travelling through the Flinders Ranges. Closer to Adelaide, the scenery changes, becoming fertile and green. We pass through the outskirts of a town, and out in the corridor, where I have been standing to stretch my legs, I can see the back yards of weatherboard houses, with utes on the back streets.

***

Adelaide is a city of about one million—(outside Sydney and Melbourne, most Australian state capitals are of similar sizes, give or take half a million.) It's within say, two days comfortable drive of Alice, a week's drive of Darwin, and close, in Australian terms, to Melbourne along the Great Ocean Road. It was founded in the 1830s and has planned, laid-out streets and gardens. It's also known for being a "free" state which did not take convicts and the accent has a discernible, perhaps even refined, English influence to the ear.

We arrive in the late afternoon Friday. As we're all hungry, we head over to a British-styled pub a block down, and order dinner and drinks. The first thing I notice is a schooner of beer is called a pint; ask for a schooner and you'll be disappointed.

Rebecca gets an SMS from Brett and is excited. Back to the room: without wasting time, she dashes off to shower, and dressing, changes into a new pair of jeans. We laugh as she does a little jig in the middle of the room to get into them.

Adelaide is known as the "City of the Churches", as there is one on every corner it seems, for all denominations and faiths. The Adelaide Hills can be seen from many of these corners.

I decide to visit these hills and world-renowned Barossa Valley, a wine region famous for well-known brands Jacob's Creek and other popular Australian Shiraz, Cabernet and Merlot, along with whites like Riesling. Something like 48 wineries supply approximately sixty thousand tonnes of grapes each vintage, and 25% of all wine produced in Australia.

I've signed up with a minibus tour run by Groovy Grape, for an 8am start. No need for an alarm—there are gun-shots from the range next door to the hostel as locals with the morning off let off rounds.

The guide, Jason, is witty and keeps up a tirade of banter and information from an obviously rehearsed playlist. We drive through the outskirts of Adelaide on the way to the Valley, and he tells us the story of an old woman that drove her car in to the local pub on a street corner. Evidently, she was very apologetic and helped the owners to refurbish the place, even earning herself her own barstool.

We climb in to the valley, and the scenery unfolds. The valleys roll spotted with trees and vegetation all round. Soon we arrive in the town of Tanunda, where museums, bottle shops have pride of place. The village has German influence, but at one end of it is an English sweetshop. We crowd in, and can see Fox's glacier mints, sherbet dips, cosmic dust and other treasures from our childhood. A backpacker and I stand outside, sucking and slurping, and several girls giggle.

"Honestly! Seeing two grown-up men eating sweets and sucking on lollies looks so strange," one says.

The first vineyard we pull up in is Orlando, home to Jacob's Creek, where a purpose-built visitors' centre has been built to pander to the curiosity of tourists keen to inspect the home of one of Australia's most famous exports. Tasting is at a bar in a glass-fronted area the height of an aircraft hangar, with commanding views. There are jugs of water, but most backpackers pass on that.

We move on to Richmond Grove, a vineyard centred in a chateau on a river. Whilst we discharge our duties in the cellar, Jason is preparing the bar-b-que in the garden outside. We sit at picnic tables in high spirits, and try kangaroo steak which turns out to be lean and gamey. Jason grabs a football from somewhere, and myself and an Irishman—the tourists—play Jason and another Australian in the group. It's quite a change for me to be playing the "beautiful game". The girls watch from the grass and encourage us.

"Come on Beckham," they shout at us. "Bend it!"

Our final stop is at Tarac Distillery, but on the way, we pull over at Menglers Hill, a popular viewpoint overlooking the valley. Tarac is a twee cottage sited on a hillside enveloped with trees. I am reminded of a view over the Rodborough valley in Gloucestershire, where my friend Katrina has a cottage.

Later, sitting in the combined bar and canteen, and over a generous portion of apple pie and ice cream, I get talking to two Irish girls, one a blonde, the other dark. They are fun and flirty, and they invite me to call around to their room. As soon as I come through the door, the blonde one says:

"OK! Take your clothes off. We're having you now."

"Yup," says the dark-haired girl. "Take them off."

Steady on girls. The girls chat incessantly, and I get a photo of them both wearing Australian bush hats, arms around each other, broad cheeky grins on their faces. The dark-haired girl is particularly friendly, with an impish face and an uncanny resemblance to the singer Bjork. An hour or so later, I am lying on the sofa in the TV room with Bjork. She is lying in my lap, and when the others leave, I turn over and kiss her. She responds, opens her eyes, and grins at me wickedly.

***

Before leaving Adelaide, I meet up with Rebecca from the train in Glenelg, a beach resort there, and she updates me about Brett, she has moved in with him.

We spend a day in the Shark Museum, the museum operated by Rodney Fox, a well-known, infamous even, Australian who was attacked by a Great White Shark in 1963 off the Adelaide coast, suffered horrific injuries, yet survived. Once bitten, not quite perturbed, he spent the rest of his life interested in sharks, and the pioneering techniques he and his wife used to discover shark behaviour were put to use in the filming of Spielberg's *Jaws* in the 1970s.

I board the train on Tuesday evening, onwards to Kalgoorlie, and we take all day Wednesday—perhaps not quite as alluring as I thought it might be—to cross the Nullarbor. The Nullarbor

(Latin for no tree) plain is featureless, apart from miles and miles of stunted bushes. It is traversed by the Eyre Highway, linking eastern and western Australia, only sealed in 1976. The Great Victoria Desert bounds the north of the plain and the Southern Ocean the south.

As we cross the 100th degree of latitude, a recorded train announcement tells us a full 99 per cent of South Australia's population lives east of that line; scarcely one percent lives west of it. We pull past a corrugated tin house with outhouses. A man called Shaggy lived here, working on the railway for all his working life. He had no visitors save for four trains going past a week, and only his dog, chickens, and sheep for company. A section of track is the longest straight track in the world, about 300 miles in length. When we finally approach a bend at about 4.30pm in the afternoon, this is announced, and we can feel a new sensation as the train leans in to the corner.

We pull in to a ghost town called Cook with a population of two—a husband and wife team run a souvenir shop there. We get off the train and wander listlessly around in 35 degrees around derelict weatherboard houses, past a closed filled-in swimming pool until we get to the shop. The shop is bustling with people purchasing postcards, tea-towels, beer mats, maps and mugs. Ten years ago, the town was home to about ten thousand people, but the privatisation of Southern Railways in the early 1990s soon changed that.

We cross over to Western Australia; its main claim to fame is it doesn't have daylight saving because if it did, "all the men would get erections on the bus on the way to work." The local time zone is now two hours behind Sydney.

The train is due in at Kalgoorlie at about eight o'clock tonight. So, I wander aimlessly around, shuttling between my seat where I read, and the lounge car with card games in progress. I get chatting to two blokes: one is an Australian from Queensland called Ian, the other is an American, Dan, a medical technician.

Ian is a retired Australian Special Air Service Colonel who joined the army as a young man and worked his way up through the ranks, getting his helicopter pilot's licence along the way. His service pension finances annual round trips of choice around Australia and the ability to buy his daughter—a Japanese interpreter—and his son, a junior SAS officer currently serving in Afghanistan–BMWs every few years.

He grew up in the regions, and describes the relationship between the indigenous population and landowners. When he was fifteen, back in the 1950s, his father caught a young Aboriginal stealing from him. He found the fella pushing a dead lamb he had stolen in to a bush for retrieval later that night. His father shot him in the leg, called the police, and the local sheriff locked the man up and thanked his father for his help.

He recounts a story of when his father went away, leaving instructions to shoot vermin in the barn. Ian went out most nights and shot bats and rats, and when his father returned and inspected the barn in the day, gazed at light beams slotting through tens of holes in the roof.

When the train slows at about 8pm, we see lights from mining operations on the outskirts of Kalgoorlie come in to view. We disembark to find the evening balmy with a light breeze. Convenient for us: a backpacker minibus from a hostel is waiting, so I throw my rucksack on board.

CHAPTER 13 SKIMPIES AND SKIVVIES

"**I**f you want good money, get a job as an offsider, mate," says the miner.

"You need HR and a MARCSTAR," adds my new acquaintance over a schooner of Swan, blowing smoke in my direction.

I nod and try to take on board this information as it's my ticket to a new job. Offside-drilling is a much sought-after position, essentially assisting a driller, performing the physical work connected with prospecting.

It is gruelling, hot work, out in the middle of the desert goldfields and, unsurprisingly, perhaps, the turnover of personnel is high. But the pay is good–in fact, very good. Rates of 250–400 dollars a day are not unusual. My new friend delivers these details through slurred speech and my alcohol-riddled haze, but I ascertain later that HR is an Australian "Heavy Rigid" truck driving licence, and the MARCSTAR is a miners and reconstruction contractor's "safety" training certificate.

I am sitting on a bar stool in a hotel in Kalgoorlie, Western Australia—or "WA" as it is referred to—called the Swan, speaking to a local miner sat next to me. Kalgoorlie is one of two things to the casual backpacker: either a desert jewel and prosperous gold-mining town awash with well-paid work in the WA desert; or a dump of a place serving as a rest stop on the twice-weekly three-day journey from Sydney to Perth.

And "Kal", as it is known to the locals, is also a frontier town that wouldn't be out of place in an American Western, and its reputation has been built on gold, founded by Paddy Hannan in 1893. It is famous for the mile-long, and hundreds of metres deep, Super-Pit, an amalgamation of the town's collection of gold mines. Huge mining vehicles operate the pit, each one the size of several houses, which make the Toyota Land Cruisers next to them look like toy cars.

Twenty years ago, the town had a reputation for rowdiness, and it was not unusual for miners and workers to spill out on to the pavement at chucking out time, or to brawl over the skimpies who work in the numerous bars that feature down the wide main street.

Skimpies are an essential part of the town's business: earning a living serving miners in skimpy outfits which amount to see-through bikini bras, and g-strings that leave little to the imagination. Not so long ago, local council regulations dictated they must wear satin veils to hide their modesty, but most skimpies arrange them so miners can still get a good eyeful. Before then, girls could choose to go topless, and I haven't been able to ascertain the truth in the story I heard twenty years ago they served in next to nothing (probably not true.) The goal of a skimpy is to sell—the more a miner drinks, the more he is likely to tip her; in exchange, she exposes her breasts.

However, I have not come here to ogle skimpies, I am sounding out work opportunities before the next Indian Pacific leaves here on Saturday in three days. Ian has agreed to collect me in his 4x4 at the station when the train arrives in Perth on the Sunday morning, so I'm sorted. I'm booked in to a hostel on Hay Street.

The miner and I leave with his mates, and we head straight up the main street, Hannan Street, to The Exchange, a popular bar on the corner of Hannan Street and Boulder Road, with a connecting door to the outfit next door, an Irish theme bar called Paddy's where we spot Skimpies.

One girl is very slim and lithe, wearing a white g-string and see-through bra, and another girl, rather more buxom, serves an indifferent miner. Still, there is as much flesh on display at Bondi beach. I spend the next few hours with my ears pinned back, trying to get the measure of the place, taking in all around me: there is a kind of "anything goes" atmosphere.

Around midnight, I head back to the hostel, on Hay Street. The two hostels in town are in a prime location opposite the town's famous brothels—a catchment area if you like.

I amble past one. It is housed in what looks like a freshly painted pink and red shed, with tacky neon signs, with about eight doorways leading through in to bedrooms. The girls are either sitting quietly in their rooms, or they are standing brazenly in their doorways. About 100 yards further on down the road, another brothel is touting for business. A bored receptionist is sitting at her desk in the lobby. This is the "mid-end" of the market.

The final brothel, right opposite my hostel, is well-appointed, and looks more like a country club and advertises tours. For ten bucks you can go in and have a beer and play pool with the girls. Armed with a little Dutch courage, I enter. It is decorated and furnished in the style of an old gentleman's London club straight out of Belgravia, WC1. Wall-mounted paintings lend an air of civility and tradition, and comfy, deep, leather sofas surround a pool table, where three girls sit demurely, their legs crossed.

There is one patron here, a young fella about 25, who is drinking and sitting talking quietly to the girls. I sit next to a raven-haired beauty, who is wearing a yellow dress. The young fella nods and asks me if I am new in town. I explain I am interested in offsider work, and he tells me he's in the same line of business himself, pulling up his sleeves to reveal sinewy arms and well-developed muscles.

"Yup, it's a hard yakka, mate," he says.

We talk and the girls look bored and perhaps a mite put out. I turn my attention to the girl in the yellow dress, and we chat, and I admit I am not in here, for shall we say, "business", but to relax a bit and have a chat. This does not annoy her, and she opens up about her work. She tells me she gets job satisfaction from performing a service. I am impressed by this revelation, as it is all too easy to assume there is an underhand reason into such a lifestyle: a different perspective of the oldest profession in the world.

She asks if I want a free tour of the brothel. My time's up, but as it's quiet tonight, her manager gives us the nod. The brothel has about fifteen bedrooms, and each one is decorated expensively in a different theme. In one there is a bed modelled on a convertible car, and another is modelled in colonial Victorian—"adult mischief meets Disney Land" I think. I bid her goodnight, telling her I will return the following evening. She nods understandingly, and says:

"I suppose you want to do it with more oomph," and she makes a putting gesture with her right arm—like she's breaking at a pool table.

***

I'm walking to the offices of the drilling company to investigate jobs before it gets seriously hot–and we haven't hit summer. The office in Boulder, a satellite suburb of Kalgoorlie, used to be a separate town but has since been swallowed up by the growing sprawl. It was originally the miner's camp on the edge of the Mile.

All roads are wide in Kal, stemming from the days when camel trains used the width to turn around in before the introduction of the motorcar.

The girl on reception is young, and sports a mild case of acne but the way her eyes flit from her monitor and to a sheet of copy propped up beside, tell me she has more pressing things to be concerned about. She tells me the manager I need to speak to is in a meeting. I am in luck, as he agrees to speak to me. He comes out into reception armed with a portfolio in his arms and gives me an address for a school. Thanking him, I stand on a corner beside a statue of a miner and collect my thoughts.

It is now getting very hot—probably approaching 40 degrees, and I would be mad to walk back to Kal in those conditions, so I decide to hitch. I face back towards town, extending my hand. I'm not too sure what the protocol is in Australia for hitching, but I'll get by. I wait and watch the endless line of utes and cars pass by. A navy-blue Holden Commodore pulls up. I get in and see the driver is on his phone, so I mouth:

"Kal."

We pull away, and head back in to Kal by another route. The man is dressed in shirt and tie and appears to be discussing prices and schedules. We pull up next to the Exchange, at the lights, and I motion to the driver I am going to get out as the lights are on red. He puts down his phone for a moment, and says,

"Thanks, mate. Sorry about that."

He is most apologetic.

"No, thank *you* mate," I say.

I head over to the driving school. The receptionist tells me driving instruction is 130 bucks an hour. This seems steep. She also tells me I will need a truck learner's permit granted after a theory test at the local Road Traffic Authority–back in Boulder, where I have just come from.

With a certain weariness, I hitch-hike back, this time, getting a lift in seconds. I am walking along Boulder Road, arm and hand extended, and a car screeches to a halt, inches from me; the driver so keen to help he almost runs me over.

I discover I need to start off with a WA driving licence so pass over my UK licence before sitting a first test.

I grab a copy of the Western Australian Highway Code from amongst a stack of *Cosmopolitan*s and *Marie-Claire*s on a stand, and study it for ten minutes, paying particular attention to the right of way rules at intersection. I sit the test at the computer, passing.

For the permit, I then memorise the 20 questions on driving trucks relating mostly to the carriage of loads, and maximum dimensions of trucks—that sort of thing. The supervisor selects the test from a menu, and I answer the ten questions—again, getting the test result back instantly—10/10. I conclude the session by composing myself for a photo which is married up to a credit-card sized WA licence.

Back at the hostel, I bump in to a tall, blonde girl walking around with her left hand in plaster. She explains how she got the injury.

She got a game of pool with backpackers from the train, and first up, set to break. The cue had a massive splinter in it, though, and she put the entire shard through the web of her supporting hand. They whisked her to hospital with the cue through her hand, and the splinters were removed in theatre the next day.

Buoyed by this amusing story, I decide in Perth I'll find out how much driving instruction is there as I'm headed that way soon. I call Southern Railway and book the next train leaving Kalgoorlie on Saturday night.

Tired after my exertions in Boulder, I lay low, taking the next morning easy. We mope around in the hostel, and hang out in the sun. A line of ants marching by in different directions on the tarmac next to the fence on closer inspection turns out to be a complete circle around the hostel ground. We are joined by an Aboriginal man who travels around the country demonstrating to school children his culture. He gives us a display—singing to us, cross-legged on the ground and accompanying himself on percussion instruments and a digeridoo. His voice and rhythm are excellent, and he builds up from a speaking pace to a fast-rap song, with a chorus.

After lunch, I bump in to an Englishman, Barry, who is the proud owner of a real bargain Toyota ute. He found it in a car yard in Darwin, and the vehicle has served him well over thousands of kilometres along outback dirt roads. He is going to pay a visit to the Super-Pit and museum on the outskirts of town, so I join him.

We arrive at Hannan's North Historical Mining Complex and descend in a lift in to an old disused mine, where a friendly, zippy Australian girl takes us through an invigorating tour down in the depths. We follow her in to a corner of the mine.

"Well," she says, looking around, "are we all here?"

She tells us a story about the methods of drilling used when this pit was open, and points at a huge pneumatic drill in the corner.

"The miners used to wait hours for parts sometimes, but

this is WA–'Wait Awhile', and it was no better in the Northern Territory–'Not Tuesday', 'Not Thursday', 'Not Today'!"

Everyone laughs. She invites us to put our hands over our ears, and she turns on the drill, which makes a racket in the confined space.

We emerge back up top and go over to a wooden hut to see gold being poured. There are seats set out for watchers behind a rope-fenced section. A pair of blokes dressed in safety gear and visors demonstrate the pouring of the gold ingot. One remarks on today's market price and allows us to draw our own conclusions on much money we are looking at. He then tells us we have just witnessed the pouring of a brass bar. (The real McCoy would entail far more security. You can witness a genuine pour at Fort Knox in San Francisco.)

In the museum, I wander over to the drilling sections, trying to find out as much as I can about drilling, hungry for information. I get talking to an older, rather shrivelled looking curator who tells me about mining life in the 1960s and takes me around. By studying the photos on the exhibits, I try to find information that will give me an understanding of the job involved.

Barry drives us over to the Super-Pit lookout, just off the Eastern Bypass Road near Boulder. A platform grants views in to the pit, and we're expecting a demolition to take place promptly at 2pm. When a while has passed, and there are no sounds or signs of explosion, we realise it must have been cancelled, which happens when the wind is blowing in the direction of town, or the conditions are unfavourable—the mining companies aren't silly.

Perhaps the mining companies will employ me once I have that truck licence, so I head west for Perth.

CHAPTER 14 TESTING TIMES IN PERTH

O n Sunday morning, I arrive in Perth, and sure enough, as promised, Ian is waiting for me at the station, standing on the platform as the Indian Pacific pulls in. He grabs my pack, and escorts me out in to the carpark to his British racing green Nissan 4x4. It turns out he has got himself a serviced apartment in Belmont, near Ascot racecourse.

"It's good, Steve, wait until you see it," he says, chatting away.

Ian gives me a quick run around Perth, an unusual city in that it is one of the most remote cities on Earth–any tourist will tell you it is closer to Singapore than Sydney. With a population of one and a half million, it often turns up in "best lifestyle" categories in top world-city lists. It is where the Australian entrepreneur, Alan Bond, first made his impact, but locals are happy to live more subdued lives on the public beaches. It's also popular with English expats seen around town in Man United tops. (Pick your club.) There's a tiny little piece of domestic trivia: I've been led to believe houses are built on sand, so feature double-brick construction rather than the brick veneer out east.

Perth has seen mining booms come and go over the years, and it's about to take off again. Residents work shifts out in the regions as "Fly-In Fly-Out" workers returning to the city between each shift.

We approach a highway bridge over the railway line and we can see the entire CBD skyline. It is surprisingly small; no bigger than a country town. Ian skirts through the CBD, and we drive past along the river, to King's Park, overlooking West Perth and the river. He pulls up in an observation site, and we take in the view.

Thus orientated, we drive to Northbridge, a popular destination for backpackers, just north of the central railway line which cuts through the CBD, for a spot of breakfast, and find a trendy café. Ian orders eggs, tomatoes, bacon, sausages and mushrooms with a serve of toast. I have eggs and toast. We share a pot of coffee and tea. Ian fills me in on the whereabouts of Dan, who shot off to Cottesloe when they arrived.

At Cottesloe beach, a north-western suburb of Perth, Dan is nowhere to be seen, so we head back to the flat. It's in an apartment block with two bedrooms; a master bedroom Ian has occupied, and a twin, which I take. There is an equipped kitchenette and laundry-bathroom. I can't believe my luck.

Popping out to a food court, Ian buys a dinner of KFC, a salad from the grocery, and a six-pack of beer, and refuses to take any contribution for it. With the TV on, in between bites, the conversation turns to his Australian SAS days. I think back to a bloke called Paul in my cousin's office block on the Central Coast, who told me he served around the same time.

"Do you know a guy called Paul Jenson by any chance?" Ian thinks for a while.

"He'd be quite a talkative bloke," I add.

A broad grin spreads across Ian's face.

"Yeah–I remember him."

Back in the late 1960s, they were training out in Northern Australia in the Tropics and out one day on a river, Paul continued his penchant for baiting crocodiles with hand grenades tied to pieces of wood. It was all too easy—the crocodiles took the grenade which then exploded inside them.

"You should have seen it, Steve," laughs Ian.

***

Ian and I have been intrigued by goings-on in the flat upstairs. There have been people arriving and leaving. Blokes traipse the stairs at odd hours, and they are not the same people. Ian has seen a single young woman leaving the flat, driving a beat-up Datsun. He voices his suspicions.

"I reckon she's a working girl, Steve," he ventures.

Ian drops me off in Northbridge in the morning, and I call the local driving schools from a public phone box outside the state reference library. A company in Mannington, south-east of the city, charge at 65 bucks an hour—half the price of Kalgoorlie. I am so delighted by this good fortune, so when I look up and see a girl smiling at me from the other phone, I strike up a conversation with her. She has an oversized envelope in her hand, and it turns out she has been ringing photo-editors at Perth newspapers to sell photos of the aftermath of the Bali bombings. She is a newly started freelance photo-journalist. Her name is Nigella.

"Want to go for a drink, Nigella?"

"Sure!" she replies, "Let's go to Dome."

She points over to a coffee shop on the corner.

Nigella has just pulled out her photos and I crane forward just in time to see a car turn from a side street, against the right of way—and collide with a removal van. There is a screech of tyres and tinkling of a breaking headlight. Nigella and I are first on the scene. A woman is lolling in the driver's seat, moaning incoherently. Despite her seat belt, she has cracked her head on the windscreen, and already an egg-sized bump is coming up on her forehead. The front of her car is a complete mess. The driver of the small truck, and his offsider, is unhurt. A waiter from Dome gets into the car behind the woman and supports the back of her head. Soon the police and the ambos arrive on the scene. I am monitoring the woman's condition when I hear my name called.

"Steve!"

Ian has arrived to pick me up as arranged. He has a bemused look on his face. Nigella and I give our eyewitness accounts, and the police take her contact details, and not mine, as she will be around to give evidence to the insurance company when I'm long gone.

When the emergency crews leave, and the woman has been taken to the ambulance, the three of us head over to a food court. Over a Chinese, Ian updates me with what he's learnt. Apparently, he has bumped into the girl from next door in the

Northbridge underground carpark and in a fit of curiosity, asked if she was a working girl. She said yes, she was, and quick as a flash, asked if he was a cop. Ian joked with her and then put me in it by saying he would send me around.

"She's cheap, mate," he states evenly.

Ian drives me over to Mannington only fifteen minutes drive away, but we get lost on the highways in Perth. We circle the area looking for the school, but we find it, and notice I am still in time for my 9am appointment.

My instructor is waiting by the truck, an American style 'snouted' ten-tonne prime-mover with a ten-tonne concrete load on the back. I climb into the cab and am at once confronted with the intricacies of the 13 speed Ranger gearbox.

Pulling away, I start in three, and change to four, like in a car. I then flick a switch which takes me into the next range of gears, moving into five, six, seven and eight for cruising. It's not too bad, but I must double-declutch the gearbox when changing up, and when changing down must blip the throttle in between to match the engine speeds to the transmission. It takes a bit of fancy footwork. The entire rig has a fair bit of inertia, so I need to allow plenty of distance to stop.

He is laid-back though, and I am rewarded with a litany of "That's the Go!" and "She'll be right!"

Feeling rather pleased after my first lesson, we head to popular Scarborough beach. On the way back, in traffic, we see a Ford station wagon ahead of us for sale: priced at $850. I know a bargain when I see one—backpacker Fords of a similar age go for around $2000 dollars, so I call the mobile number advertised, and when the seller pulls up, offer $700 which he accepts. I can drive to truck lessons and sell—making a profit—before I leave Perth.

***

I'm at the WACA—the Western Australian Cricket Association, the Perth Cricket stadium, in East Perth to watch the opening match on the current Ashes tour—England the visitors, or "touring" side of course. There will be five test matches in Brisbane, Adelaide, Perth, Melbourne and Sydney, and as I continue on the road, I might be able to see a match in person, or catch it on TV. I spend the morning lazing in the stands, idly watching Langer, an emerging Aussie cricketer, taking wickets. I explain to an American the rules of cricket (as best I can.)

Back at the apartment, I stroll around, fixing myself a cup of tea, and sandwiches—and notice a note from Ian pinned to the fridge. He explains he has had to return to Queensland, as his daughter has been bitten by a brown snake, and that he has put his 4x4 into storage at Perth domestic airport. However, as the rent is paid up to the end of the week, I might as well stay there and make use of it.

I go back to the car for my sunnies and bump into a girl coming towards me through the alleyway. It's the working girl. She follows me back towards my door, and asks:

"Are you Ian's mate. Do you know where he is?"

"Yeah–he's gone to Queensland. Left this morning."

I flash the note from my back pocket.

She invites me into her flat. I tell her about being able to stay in the flat until the end of the week, which is good, as it gives me a chance to take my driving test. She is an artist and shows me her scrapbooks with sketches, and prints mounted on the wall. She offers me the chance to stay, helping her with rent money.

"But–you'd have to go and hide in the bathroom or other bedroom, or something, when I have guests," she adds.

What a proposal. Flat-sharing offers from a working girl. She lights a joint and smokes it and I saunter back downstairs, passing by a client. Down in the flat, I hear the creak of bedsprings and their sighs and gasps through the narrow walls. Finally, there is a grunt and a short while later, there are the sound of steps back down the stairs.

My tenure over, I drive over to party central Northbridge back across the Swan River and check into the Ozi Inn on Newcastle

Street, a main west-east artery full of hostels. The Ozi Inn is a converted house where rooms cost 11 bucks a night. Pubs and clubs are a block away, and I am introduced to Perth nightlife. I bump into a bloke I met in Adelaide, a tall, skinny northerner with a striking resemblance to one of the singers from the English 1980s group The Housemartins, get talking to two Welsh girls from Cardiff.

Test day dawns, and finds me toying with my breakfast in a small café opposite the school, steadying my nerves by skimming through the car adverts in the local paper. My instructor turns up outside with the truck.

H-hour.

The test starts well enough, and I relax by telling the examiner I am angling for a job in the mines (maybe he will go easy) but that doesn't stop him marking his paper with an "X" at an intersection. An outright fail? I continue to drive nervously around the course. Along the way, I pick up more "X"s and I wonder if I was ready. To make things worse, I miss the entrance of the test centre, and need to reverse and turn around in a driveway. I am not sure I can salvage much from this test.

My instructor walks over, and the examiner winds down the window, and asks:

"How many hours has he had?"

"About five," he replies.

Twist the knife mate. I make faces of helplessness at him.

"Well, he's only just got it," remarks the examiner, climbing out.

I stare unbelievingly at his departing back.

"X"s are for minor faults: one more, and I would have failed.

Relieved, I visit King's Park with the Welsh girls in their Scooby Doo camper van, and we spend an afternoon lounging around on the cropped grass by the war memorial. It's a popular destination, and the entire city is laid out before us in the spring sunshine. The quiet before the storm—as the annual premier event on the racing calendar, the 142nd Melbourne Cup, is about to get underway.

The entire city—and country for that matter—has been working to a go-slow that morning and comes to a standstill whilst the race is on. The pubs are full of people who have taken their lunch hours—and the rest of their day—off to party. To me and many backpackers, it is a disappointment: the Grand National eclipses it surely for excitement and entertainment, and as a contest. Expecting an odyssey of stamina and skill, we find the race lasts barely two minutes. Damien Oliver wins the 3,200 metre race on Media Puzzle; scant consolation as his brother was killed the week before in horse trials at Ascot.

At a loose end, I take the train a few stops from Northbridge to Leederville and find a large fish restaurant and market at the bottom of a bridge that crosses the railway line. I walk into the market, where I am confronted with racks of fresh fish of all shapes and sizes. I ask one of the assistants if he can tell me anything about the supply chain as I am interested in crew jobs on fishing or shrimping boats out on the north-west Australian coast. A colleague of his explains we are out of season, but explains the towns of Carnarvon, and Exmouth would be my best bet.

**

Before getting on the train on Friday morning, I sell my car to a Scotsman, who gives me my asking price. We both walk away pleased: I've turned a profit, and he has saved paying over the odds. At the station, I bump into a girl I met in Adelaide who is soon to start training with the Royal Navy. In the lounge car, she and I play a brain-teaser card game with a Danish girl with dark cropped hair and striking blue eyes.

We arrive back in Kal that same evening. Paul and his wife at GoldDust Backpackers are a friendly couple and are good for work opportunities—I explain that I am over for drilling vacancies. The hostel is nice, with a convivial family atmosphere. The owners keep an eye on everyone, and make sure people get put forward for jobs.

Saturday afternoon, I am lying by the pool, relaxing in the sun, popping inside every so often to look at the action from the First Test from Brisbane. Paul tells me a driller has phoned the hostel looking for offsiders.

At 6pm, Grant arrives in a brand-new gunmetal grey Toyota Land Cruiser and sits next to me on the bench outside where we are joined by another job seeker from the hostel.

Grant has just got back from Melbourne from a wedding, and he is feeling a little crook as a result—*go easy on me*, he seems to say. He is wearing a fawn buttoned shirt and a pair of smart shorts. He is a handsome man, with boyish rugged looks, medium length hair and twinkling blue eyes which he directs at us in turn, in a steady gaze. A working life of drilling has left him sturdy and fit. He speaks in an even, gravelly voice.

"OK boys. I'm looking for two offsiders, but I can only take one of you two, as I've already promised one vacancy to a bloke who's coming over from Perth on the train."

He explains the job is very physical, in fact he is going to take us over to his yard to see the drill we will be operating to give us an idea what we are in for. Another thing: drug-taking; mining companies regularly test for levels in the bloodstream of miners, we had better be clean.

We jump in the front seats of the Cruiser, and we drive off down the main road of Kal to an industrial area. We turn into a yard enclosed by a mesh fence. He pulls up next to a truck with a huge drill, lying in its horizontal position. We get out, and the other bloke from the hostel lights a cigarette and we contemplate the truck.

"The Air Core Drill," announces Grant. "It's a type of Reverse Circulation Drill."

Grant indicates three-metre long rods, six inches wide, each weighing about 45 kilogrammes. The rods are called "Air Core", as inside each rod is a smaller "inner-tube" of metal where air can expand.

"This is the crux of the job. You've got to lift the rods from this rack–" he presses a button, and the drill raises from horizontal to an angle pointing down, then gestures to the ground–"to a position in line with the drill so you can connect it."

He regards us, looking for our reaction. The bloke from the hostel draws on his cigarette. I try to look impassive.

"See if you can lift a rod. You go first, mate."

I step forward and drag out a rod from the stack. It is bloody heavy—you would want to locate the rod into the drill bit as soon as possible, as any manoeuvring would exhaust you. I continue to hold it in midair for a while, and Grant helps me set it back. He looks half impressed but switches back to impassive.

He turns and looks at the bloke from the hostel, who has just stubbed out his cigarette. He steps forward and lifts the rod as well, and I crane forward, competitively, looking to see if he finds it any easier. Outwardly he looks no different, but he exclaims:

"**** it's heavy!" and sets it down promptly.

"OK," says Grant. "See what I mean? It's heavy. You'll be doing that every minute for perhaps 40 minutes at a time. Remember, it's hot out there."

We step away from the truck, and Grant continues to direct his steady gaze at first one of us, then the other, as he talks, seemingly looking for any uncertainty or weaknesses.

"Have you both got HR?" he asks.

We nod, myself with an element of pride. This is the second time he has asked.

"Have you got First Aid?" he asks next.

The bloke from the hostel nods.

"I was a first aid instructor," I say which is true.

Grant nods, absorbing this new information. He explains once more how difficult the job is.

"I want to see you lift it again."

I move first—this seems to impress Grant as the bloke from the hostel looks away and lights another cigarette. He looks at us again.

"Remember–it's nasty and hot out there, boys."

Grant says he will let us know tomorrow.

"And–stay off the piss guys!" he adds.

I'll go easy, but there's a night out to come.

I prepare an omelette, next to an Australian girl from Sydney with a withered hand. England are playing New Zealand at Twickenham. Ireland are hosting Australia in Dublin. I am particularly looking forward to the autumn internationals at Twickenham this year; the Kiwis have sent a team for the first time since 1997. England relishes the chance to play them at home, as the opportunities seem so few and far between. It's all good prep for the 2003 World Cup, in any case. The girl from Sydney asks if she can come. The more the merrier.

We go over to The Exchange, and over beers, watch Australia play Ireland in our first fixture. Historically, the Wallabies lose, and this hasn't happened since the 1970s. We move over to Paddys, next door, to watch the England-New Zealand game. The game is tight, and in the closing minutes, England is holding on to a narrow lead. I find myself on the dance floor edge. A girl is there, also watching avidly. When England win at the final whistle, she groans.

"A kiwi, eh," I gloat.

"I know! It's bloody terrible," she replies.

"First time at Twickenham in almost ten years," I remind her.

My Sydney companion is sweet, and back in the accommodation in the vacant kitchen she looks over her shoulder and turns around for a kiss.

***

I am playing cards with a bunch of Kiwis, and Paul calls me over to the phone. I pick up the receiver.

"Hello?" I say.

"Is that Steve?" replies a man's voice.

"Er, yes, it is."

"It's Grant here. Do you still want the job?"

"Yes..."

"You're the Englishman, aren't you?" he asks checking once more.

"Yes," I state for the record.

"OK, you've got the job. In the end it came down to the fact your first aid experience was better than the other guy's."

"Thanks mate, that's great. I've got my course this afternoon," I reply.

"Great. Ok, this is what I need you to do. Meet me outside this evening, with your documentation, tax file number and driving licences. Now could you get me the other bloke so I can give him the bad news?"

I find Paul. He tells me I got the job when Grant rang the hostel asking for references. My competitor drinks too much, and he told Grant so. Meanwhile, the other offsider arrives from Perth and checks in; he's a big bloke–I can't see him having any difficulties.

I saunter over to the office of a company that conduct MARCSTAR courses. There's a round of lectures in a room with formica tables and a rotating line of instructors who take us through modules. The slides are often horrendous, even rather amusing: overloaded, upturned trucks, ladders upended and hazardous spills. I am walking back to the accommodation with my course pass, and bump into Grant cruising down the road. He takes my documentation.

"You got boots Steve?"

I don't have any, so he whisks me over to a work gear shop and buys me shorts, bright fluoro shirt and metal-capped boots all on the company account. He's a good bloke.

"See you outside tomorrow–4.30am." He adds:

"By the way, I sent the guy from Perth packing. He didn't have any paperwork. We're taking my cousin instead."

CHAPTER 15 IT MUST SURELY BE THE HARDEST JOB IN THE WORLD

I'm outside for 4.20am, as promised, and am ready packed with a daysack. I'm ten minutes early, leaving nothing to chance. It is pleasantly cool, after the scorching heat of the Kalgoorlie day with the promise of heat to return. Sunrise is 6am. Grant turns up. After a short drive to an outer suburb, we pick up the other offsider. His name is Nick. He is about 20, around six foot, wiry with a teenager's build.

At the yard, we make final preparations. We manhandle the sample cyclone on to the trailer hitched to the drill truck. I stand on the back of the trailer, and take the weight of the cyclone as Grant and Nick bump it up the ramp. Seeing Grant securing one side down with lengths of rope, I secure the other, using a somewhat dubious choice of knot as my anchor. Grant glances at it and remarks:

"Where'd you work, a fish and chip shop?"

He re-ties the knot and pronounces the cyclone secure.

"Can you drive a manual?" asks Grant.

Bloody hell, I think, *he's so suspicious*. Firstly, I'm a European, and secondly, I've got HR—of course I can drive a bloody manual. If any of us can, it's me.

"You've got the Land Cruiser, then, Steve," he says.

I get in the cab and carefully reverse it out of the yard.

We've got a three-hour drive ahead of us to Leonara, a mining service town 400km away. Grant will drive the drill truck, Nick is going to drive the support and equipment truck, a "Medium Rigid" class white truck, and I'll bring up the rear in the Land Cruiser, this suits me as they're a pleasure to drive with their gutsy 4.2 litre diesel engines.

We drive out of the outskirts of Kal as light breaks over the horizon, following the main highway that heads North out to the goldfields. Just after sunrise, we pull into a servo and fill our tanks with diesel. There's a brief flap as I get the fuel nozzle stuck in the side tank of the MR truck and in getting it out, splash fuel on the tarmac. As we pull out of the servo, Grant's voice comes over clear on the CB radio in the cab.

"You on channel, Nick?"

"Yup," he replies.

I scramble for the mike nestling on the dashboard. I want to be ready when Grant contacts me.

"You on channel, Steve?" he asks seconds later.

"Yup," I reply.

Now the bugger's satisfied.

The drive to Leonora is taken at the pace of the slowest truck: Grant's drilling truck towing the trailer. I bring up the rear of the convoy, enjoying the solitude and the quiet. Twenty minutes out of Kal we are out in WA bush with the sun still very low on the horizon, illuminating the road in a red, golden glow.

It's the first time I have driven on any bush road, and it's unremarkable for a main highway, one lane of tarmac in both directions. The road is flanked with low scrub and stunted trees. Every so often, we come across roadkill; wallabies, kangaroos, even the occasional cow, which has been hit by a road-train travelling at night. There's an element of risk driving in a car or small ute at night, as a collision with a cow could have dire consequences for both parties. Dusk is a particularly poor time as wildlife comes out to feed at sundown. Crows and other wildlife swarm over the corpses and scamper away as we approach. There's occasional traffic in the opposite direction, mostly old Fords, or utes, and a police car.

About an hour into the trip, Grant pulls over in the servo yard at a township called Menzies. We pull over behind. I get out and amble over, joining Nick and Grant, who, kneeling forward, elbows on hips, is studying one of his wheels.

"Flat tyre," grumbles Grant.

We use precious time to grab a spare wheel out the back of the Land Cruiser, jack up the truck, and manhandle the nuts off the wheel with the flat tyre. Grant gets the socket set bar out of the toolbox as the nuts have locked tight. Nick and I manhandle the useless wheel to the LandCruiser and soon we're ready to go again.

When we arrive in Leonara, we turn left into a road right at the beginning of town. This is where the drilling company has its offices, and we need to report our arrival to the staff there. The office is a portacabin, and we pass through the main door into a large office area full of filing cabinets and diagrams and maps on the walls. It looks like a war planning room or Divisional HQ.

A man dressed in the ubiquitous Australian summer work dress of heavy-duty cotton shirt with epaulettes and collar, tough rugby-style shorts, socks and Blundstones boots greets Grant, and they chat. Nick and I hang back, making sure we don't get in the way, acting like the low-grade offsiders that we are. The organ-grinder doesn't need any help from the monkey when he's talking business. The man turns out to be our geophysicist, or "geo", and will accompany us on-site overseeing the drilling process. He pulls out a map, and in one corner is a row of marked crosses in a neat, diagonal line. These turn out to be the sites designated for drilling later this afternoon.

A girl emerges, dressed identically to the man save for her clothing is baggier on her. She wears her hair in a pony-tail, and has a friendly, confident grin.

"G'Day Grant. How u goin'?"

Grant looks up and grins. It turns out Sharon worked for Nick on a "Rotary Airblast" drill a few years previously so they're old hands. Nick tells me the rods of a RAB drill are less than half the weight of those in an air core setup.

We head back out into town. Grant goes off somewhere, leaving myself and Nick standing on a street corner, giving me a better chance to inspect our surroundings, whilst Nick rolls a cigarette.

Leonara is about the size of Walgett. Evidently, there is a community programme work afoot, as work gangs of aboriginals are digging up the southbound road. They eye us, and not altogether with friendliness. When Grant returns, with Sharon in tow, we head into the supermarket and grab essentials like soap powder, cereal, milk, bread, tea and coffee, and Nick picks up a few bottles of coke as Grant will be picking up the tab. Back in the Cruiser, Grant asks me one of his "direct" questions.

"Did you do any un-armed combat in the Army?"

***

Grant has rented a three-bedroom house on the main road into town across from a servo, so we hop over in the Toyota. It's a single-storey villa and has—hey—air-conditioning. We grab a room each, leaving Grant with the best room (the coolest!) I dump my gear in the corner by the bed, shake out my sleeping bag and have a quick rummage through the wardrobe, finding an old copy of *Picture* magazine. This is a mischievous little Aussie magazine, almost an icon; its main attraction is pictures of nubile "home" girls. They're not Playboy models, just regular girls next door. There have been recent adverts in Sydney backpacker fanzines for "photographic models", I wonder whether this is where the photographs will end up. Who knows, maybe I will recognise someone from Bondi, or Coogee beach? I flick through it and look up to see Grant standing in the doorway.

"Bought the smut then, Steve?" he chuckles.

Grant shouts us lunch, and we head out to the drilling site which is another 45 minutes further down the road out of town. We follow the geo, who leads us in his Toyota Hilux. The turnoff for the drilling field is marked by an old fuel drum, and so we turn off the bitumen on to a dirt road which leads through stunted trees and bush. We pass old holes that have already been drilled. There are neat rows of piled differently coloured dirt to the side of each one. These are older samples left for analysis.

We drive a track where only a single vehicle could pass, and find our site. Earth diggers from the mining company have created access and have cleared trees and main obstacles, but we still have to prepare the ground for the samples by raking, and hacking out tufts, roots and bushes.

We set up the drill truck, and the drill is angled with the business end pointing down at the hole. The cyclone is positioned, and we connect a hose that snakes from the drill to it so that drilled dirt will run through into buckets I have ready.

I put on my helmet, safety glasses and gloves, and we standby. Grant nods at me, gives me the thumbs-up, and starts the drill bit rotating. I have no idea what to expect. I signal my readiness and crouch low, like a scrum-half waiting for the ball to emerge from a driving scrum. Nick drags out a three-metre metal rod and lifts it in the air above his head, holding it there just long enough for the drill top and bit to locate and screw on to it. We drill about one metre into the ground, and all we get is a bit of surface soil running through into the bucket.

Grant indicates to me with outstretched arm and raised emphatic thumb that I have to swap out the bucket, so I grab it, switch another in its place and run out to the farthest corner of the prepared ground, and empty it as neatly as I can. No sooner than I'm back, I'm going again. Grant puts the drill in to reverse, and holds the first rod in position, so that the machine unscrews it from the top—(the bit is still in the soil). Nick locates the next rod, and the machine screws it back in. We can now drill another three metres down.

I empty the buckets for this rod, again working quickly, and neatly. After runs, I realise the knack is in running out the first two buckets, then the third can be taken slightly slower whilst Nick swaps out. And my fitness is paying dividends.

Then it all goes pear-shaped. We drill through water making the soil wet and heavy. It seeps up through the ground and runs around my feet making it difficult for me to run. After 40 metres, I am knackered. I can hardly see as my glasses are caked in mud, and I am filthy from wiping my muddy gloves on my shirt and back of my shorts. Nick shrugs his shoulders and grins. I realise now why the job is such a bugger. After this hole, Grant calls it a day. Looks like he used it as a dress rehearsal.

Covered in dust and mud, we head back into town to get showered and changed. Grant has arranged for us to get next day's lunch from the drilling company canteen, so we head over and enter the air-conditioned kitchen, which is like an Army mess hall. There is a choice of hot foods at a heated counter, a cart with bread, sauces, and cereals, and a side bar holding salad, cold-cuts and fruit. There's also a pudding trolley with sponges, tarts and a steaming vat of custard. We make sandwiches before stuffing tupperware boxes with hunks of melon, bananas and apples.

Grant takes us to the pub and disappears into the kitchen to get the cook to organise steak and chips to the front counter. I need no second bidding—I need to replenish. Back at the accommodation, suitably victualled, I drink a carton of protein whey drink and get an early night. Nick pops his head around the door, and asks for the *Picture* magazine, which I chuck over.

***

Awake at 4.30am. Breakfast is cereal and yoghurt, and we pile in the Cruiser. Grant grabs an iced coffee. We arrive in the field at about 7am and start our first hole. Half an hour in to the first hole, the geo arrives and watches from the air-conditioned safety and comfort of his ute. He ambles over, holding a sieve. He bends over and starts to sift through the more interesting looking soil piles I have lined up. I've worked out I have precious seconds between runs, in which to scrape out the buckets not in use so heavy wet soil doesn't accumulate and make my life harder. Better for us.

On the second hole, Grant sees that the water table is so high, we need to dig a trench system prior to starting work so that the work area does not flood. He indicates where to dig, and we grab a spade each and start digging.

"Put your back into it, mate," he observes.

It's hot work. The geo is watching from a safe distance.

You lucky bugger. After ten minutes we have a good hole, and then Grant digs a series of channels around the cyclone, around the drill hole all leading to the big hole. Marvellous engineering.

I'm feeling the pace.

We've done three holes, driving the trucks from hole to hole. Every hole requires prep and labouring. I'm dirty and tired, but still going strong, and luckily Grant has called a break for lunch.

Nick and I sink to the ground by the side of the support truck, under the shade of trees, on the empty upturned sample buckets and wolf down the sandwiches and the fruit, and gulp ice-cooled water from eskies. The temperature is mid-thirties and will peak near 40 centigrade sometime this afternoon. I want to take off my safety hat with sun-brim to cool down, but then I risk sunburn and direct exposure from the lethal rays.

We resume work and on this next hole, I have to run further —got to run twice as fast, to get the run done in the same time. It goes well at first. I'm running, trying to get there and back, in good time whilst not going stupid.

I start feeling dizzy, and by the end, I'm struggling to keep up with the drilling. I go to the side of the drill and guzzle water and pour it in to my hair. I feel a bit better already. Grant calls over:

"You're buggered, aren't you?" he asks.

"I'm a bit hot–that last hole was far," I pant.

"Come over here and sit down in the shade for a bit," he says, indicating the shaded area under the truck behind the wheel arch.

I mumble "I'll be alright" and flop down.

"We're not trying to kill our offsiders, despite what you think," Grant says.

"Appreciate it, Grant," I pant.

We've just finished the fifth hole, and I'm hot now. Grant wants to press on and drive to the next hole. I jump into the cab in the support truck next to Nick and the heat in there is unbearable. This makes me dizzy again, and it feels like my head is going to explode with all the blood I can feel pumping around in there. I sway; now my head seems to weigh a tonne. I just need water. Nick looks around in concern.

"Are you OK, Steve?"

"Yeah," I barely mouth. "Just need water, that's all."

My head is lolling.

Anyone who has experienced heat exhaustion knows the symptoms. There is absolutely nothing you can do about it.

"Are you sure you're OK?" Nick asks once more.

I notice he has thumbed the mike of his CB, so Grant up in front in the drill truck would have heard the exchange. We halt, and I almost pole-vault, I'm so desperate to get out of the stinking hot cab into the shade and get water. I land on my feet and wobble, and find the water esky again. Grant thinks I am near gone. Despite my protests, he orders me to stay in the shade again, and goes off and confers with the geo. The geo says he will have to report that I was a heat victim. Health and safety at work and all that.

Bollocks. This is all I need, I think. Nick also looks up at Grant:

"Boss, I'm not feeling great either."

The pair of us get through the last days, although each day gets harder and harder. In the mornings, my entire body is racked with pain, and stiff. Sitting on the porch pulling on my boots is particularly bad, and I've come to dread the half hour's drive to the drilling fields and the plod through the bush to the hole. Time for peace and quiet, and therefore rest, but another day will follow on the back of it. After I have washed off all the mud and grime, I fancy from looking in the bathroom mirror that I'm building muscle. After dinner, I stretch out on my bed and lie still, knowing asleep will come soon. To think that Grant was worried I might spend my leisure hours out in the local bars drinking.

At a hole, a team from the mining company arrive to watch us work. I suspect the real motive is they fancy a trip out of the office, and I can't say I appreciate them rubbernecking whilst we work. Sharon arrives, and the blokes preen, dusting the dirt off their clothes, and looking more alert.

After flirting with Grant, she comes over to me, and says "G'Day." Then, incredibly, she offers to help. I am torn between maintaining my pride—and allowing her to join me, and shrugging her off, but she is such a nice cheery girl, I agree to her help, and the hole goes by in no time. She chats to me as we work, asking me where I come from, and how I am enjoying my time in Australia. She even gives us a hand with digging. The geo maintains his watch from afar.

We head over to a residential home of one of Grant's friends. Their villa is located on a wide street, where concrete kerbs border mud pavements. (Paving stones are not used in these rural areas, something I first noticed out in Walgett.) Nick and I sit outside on the front porch steps, and crack open stubbies, whilst Nick chats to his friends. He calls us in to take delivery of a fridge Grant has been able to borrow off his mates, as he feels ours is not working very well.

I get through the last day, and after the last hole, I climb into the front of the Land Cruiser relieved. I think: never again.

The original plan called for us to drive back to Kal as soon as we got back to Leonara, but now Grant has received an invitation to a party and decides to delay the drive until the morning. This suits me fine, as I quite fancy a beer in Leonara and a look around in any case, although Nick is not so pleased as he has a girlfriend waiting for him back in Kal. Normally, Grant would wait for us to shower first, but he goes to the front of the queue, gets changed, and dashes out the door, but pops his head back in briefly:

"Boys. I've arranged a meal for you at the pub. Be there in twenty minutes."

Nick and I get cleaned up, and amble stiffly down the road to the pub, grab our steak and chips, and sit within view of the bar. A topless girl waltzes in through from the adjoining saloon bar next door.

Skimpies in Leonara! My spirits perk up; this is a welcome distraction. We finish up and go outside into the street, and back in through the saloon bar door. I am buying the drinks for Nick, as he is skint, so I catch the skimpy's eye, and she comes over.

"G'Day boys! How you going?" she asks.

"Good thanks," I reply agreeably. Nick nods.

"What can I get youse?" The Australian country dialect again.

"Two bourbon and cokes, please."

She turns away and gets the drinks.

"Here ya go, boys."

"What u doin' in Leonara?" she asks.

I laugh, shake my head, exchange a look with Nick, and say:

"The hardest bloody job in the world!" We all laugh.

At about eleven pm, Nick and I adjourn to another pub over the road where they will be showing the Australia vs England game live from Twickenham. We settle on stools, amongst the regulars, next to the bar, across from the door. The pub has all the atmosphere of a lock-in, and a skimpy hosts us. A couple of blokes I get talking to discuss her physical merits. They are united on one thing—her figure—but about her face they are not so sure:

"Oh well," says one, and adds philosophically; "you could put a bucket on her head, and swing on the handle."

That's not very nice.

Nick and I sit at the bar, and order rum and coke Bundies. The *rah-rah* comes on the television up in the corner but the sound has been left turned down. Rugby Union is not that popular a sport in Western Australia, but I know there will be locals keen to see the Poms lose regardless. The game starts well, but by the closing twenty minutes, Australia lead. Australia have not won at Twickenham since 1998. Nearing full-time, England were behind by a few points, but a well-worked try saved the day for their win.

I nurse a hangover the next day. We drive back to Kal, the three of us crammed in to the front of the Toyota Land Cruiser.

We stop briefly in Menzies, for Grant to buy an ice cream. The only thing of interest, on the drive back is a pilot car passing by which denotes an oversized load coming towards us—a huge low-loader with an outsized Super-Pit style bulldozer so wide we almost have to pull over. Grant gets on the CB, on the general channel, and asks in his gravelly voice,

"Where's that going, boys?"

The reply—in heavy bush dialect, is incoherent to me, but Grant seems to find it interesting enough, and he shrugs and replaces the mike.

Back in Kal, I jump in the ice-cold pool for a restorative swim, stroking through the water allowing it to bathe my bruises. I borrow a bike from reception and cycle over to Grant's yard and find him in the site office behind a desk where, licking his finger, he rifles through a cheque book, writes one out in a cursive script, and thanks me for my efforts.

In the hostel dining room, I find two girls, Sharon and Michelle. They are both from the Isle of Man, and a bubbly pair. I join them, and we board the next east coast-bound Indian Pacific on Monday as it heads back towards Adelaide. The aim is to get to Melbourne, but can watch the cricket in Adelaide before getting the train further south.

CHAPTER 16 BARMY ARMY &
FOUR SEASONS IN ONE DAY

On the train, the girls and I joke, giggle and chat our way across the Nullarbor all Monday night and all of Tuesday, finding everything and anything hilarious. Sitting in the lounge car, we evacuate it in minutes, as all the readers move on back to their seats.

We arrive early in Adelaide on the Wednesday, to discover there is no accommodation left, as most of the hostels are full up with legions of travellers hoping to catch the first day of the Second Test between Australia and England. Many of these fans will be the Barmy Army—the English tourers—in full strength, reducing our chances to practically zero. We arrive optimistically at a hostel, only to be turned away by the English receptionist who has acquired a very authentic Australian accent.

I see a backpacker bus cruising down the road, and run after it, like a hell-bent dog, and catch up when the driver pulls over. For worrying minutes, we wait whilst he contacts his colleagues at the hostel. He says he can get us beds, and drives us to the Adelaide Backpacker's Inn on Carrington Street.

The hostel is nice; cosy, friendly, exceptionally good value, and, they do a cracking all-you-can-eat five-dollar breakfast. I load up with eggs, tomatoes, mini-steaks, bacon and mushrooms, (several plate-fulls) and fill up bowls of Crunchy Nut cornflakes, all washed down with cups of tea. The hostel also serves (for no apparent reason other than generosity) free apple pie and custard at 9pm every night. Gets my vote.

I meet Sharon and Michelle in a bar on Mall, where they have met a friend of theirs. We stay up all night and end up in a rather seedy-looking club in the club quarter of Adelaide, where the bouncers greet us enthusiastically. Soon, we find drinks in a closed hotel, before emerging into the Adelaide dawn.

Several hours later, after a nap, leaving Michelle and Sharon in bed, both nursing hangovers, I walk down through Flinders Mall and up the main road to the Oval, overlooked by the statue of Colonel William Light. The weather is perfect. Crisp, blue skies, and the strong South Australian sun beats down mercilessly, making "Slip Slap Slop" a dead-cert today.

I can't miss the Oval, and a sizeable queue has developed by the box office. After a ten-minute wait, I buy a stands ticket and file in through the turnstile. I bypass the stands along an asphalt perimeter track up on to "The Hill", a patch of raised grass, largely taken over by the Barmy Army, encompassing much of the north end. I find a spot, leaving a small buffer. The Army are in full swing, and stand en masse in a huge huddle, beers in hand. Hardly a moment goes by without them offering up a song or ditty. They are led by a single character, beers in both hands, who has taken on the conductor role. He leads a song:

"Eeee-verywhere we go-ooo..."

(The rest join in, repeating every line:)

"People want to know
Who we are
Where we come from
So we tell them
Who we are
Where we come from
We are Eeeng-LAND
The mighty, mighty England
We are the Army
The Barmy, Barmy Army..."

He breaks into a variation on Waltzing Matilda, which is picked up by the rest.

"I shagged Matilda, I shagged Matilda, I shagged Matilda and so did my mate..."

A statuesque girl walks by on the asphalt track bordering the grass, and to get to her place, metres from me, she has to run the gauntlet past the Army. As she walks by there is complete silence from them, but one wag, audible over most of the Hill, cries:

"I see you! Shak–ing that aaass!"

The poor girl continues walking, visibly biting her teeth, and getting to her place, sinks to the ground and complains bitterly to her boyfriend.

"I've just been jeered at!" she says, indignantly, biting her lip.

Her boyfriend, not surprised one bit, replies,

"Course you have! What do you expect?"

The story on the cricket pitch is meanwhile unchanged; England won the toss and chose to bat first. It is highly unlikely they will win this test or indeed the Ashes series.

Trescothick and Michael Vaughan are the opening batting partners, facing Australia's most experienced bowlers, Ian McGrath and Jason Gillespie. Vaughan hits the ball towards Langer, who appears to catch it on the full (in midair). However, the umpire, Koertzen, is not so sure, and consults with the TV umpire. The replay shows that the ball may have hit the grass, and Vaughan stays at the crease.

Not long after, though, the first wicket falls, and Trescothick walks for 35, momentarily silencing the Barmy Army. It's not long, though, before they sing once more, this time a song sang to the tune of "A Yellow Submarine", directed very much at the Aussies:

"You all live in a convict colony, a convict colony, a convict colony, you all live in..."

The ringleader gets up again, and leads the army in "Are we Happy?":

"Are we happy?
Today is Monday
Monday is a finger day
Today is Tuesday
Tuesday' errrrghh!
Today is Wednesday

Wednesday is an Aussies day
Today is Thursday
Thursday is a thinking day
Today is Friday
Friday is for shagging sheep
Today is Saturday
Saturday's for Rugby
32-31
32-31
Today is Sunday
Sunday is a Day of prayer."

CHORUS:
"Are we happy? You bet your life we are!
Der de le de de de de de, der de le de de de de de."

(The last line is sung to the accompaniment of 360-degree spins, hands above head. The "32–31" chant is obviously a brand-new addition and can only refer to the recent rugby victory days ago.)

At the lunch break, I go out to the beer tent and buy another beer, coming back to the Hill in time to hear the Barmy Army sing the "Three dollars to the pound" song, set to the tune of "He's got the whole world in his hands". At this point, Australian nerves are nearing breaking point; the locals are not known for their singing and chanting, but a South Australian stands up, and sings, loudly:

"PAA-CCK your bags and **** off home, do-dah, DO-DAH!"

Play resumes:

Brett Lee bowls to Vaughan and after every ball, the Barmy Army call "No Ball!" This is in line with a general suspicion that Lee's disjointed bowling action is not legal. (His arm is not apparently straight, and he is thus accused of being a "chucker".) However, the Australian Cricket Board have analysed his action in slow-motion and declared it as "ridgy-didge" (genuine)

With England having amassed over 100 runs, I resume the afternoon session from the safety of a couch in the hostel

TV room where Sharon potters around repacking the contents of her rucksack. Michelle is still in bed suffering from a bit of alcohol poisoning. There's a shout from the Australian TV commentators when Vaughan goes for 177.

That night, I go down and test the free apple pie and custard served by the good-natured, genial old gentleman that picked us up on our arrival. Over steaming, second helpings, I bump in to two pretty girls and an ex-Navy warfare officer, a young and cherubic-looking officer of the watch.

Anyhow, I still plan to get to Melbourne, so I get the train on a service called the Overlander. I'll spend a week there, and then go to Sydney to meet up with my friend Dave (he of the private pilot licence in London), as I have just discovered in an email he has sent from Thailand he arrives next week.

***

Melbourne, Victoria, situated at the bottom of the bulge of southern Australia, is the most European of Australian cities, and not without good reason. It has elegant parks, architecture, restaurants, museums, galleries and theatres, and an element of sophistication that critics of Australia miss in other state capitals. Trams ply the city street and inner suburbs.

It has a long-standing rivalry between Sydney for Australia's premier city, and originally, was in the running for the Australian capital until Canberra in the Australian Capital Territory was built to house the commonwealth government and serve as the nation's Capital. It is also, as I discover, home to the largest Greek population outside Greece, and is well known for its multiculturalism. The 2001 Australian film called *Wog Boy* is a testament to this; "Wog" being a favoured term used for non-Australians—possibly stemming from "Western Oriental Gentlemen". The term "Wog" is not quite as derogatory or despicable as it is in the UK, but not pleasant, granted.

Melbourne has a reputation for easiness and friendliness,

exceeding a city of its size, and is therefore attractive to tourist and migrants alike. It is particularly popular with British migrants as the climate is more akin to the UK.

Situated as it is on the southern tip of Australia, with associated weather systems, it is also by far one of the coldest and changeable states in Australia. Not for nothing, has the weather in the city been described as "Four seasons in one day". Another familiar quip is "Queensland, beautiful one day, perfect the next. [On the other hand] Melbourne, beautiful one day–we hope."

Indeed, Victorian winters can get notoriously icy, but when I arrive at the end of spring, the day is a heady, humid-less 40 degrees, and the sun shines out of a beautiful blue cloudless sky. The train deposits me at the Spencer Station terminal, opposite the Colonial Stadium where large AFL games are played. I'm based on Elizabeth Street, at the Melbourne International Backpackers, at the bottom of an office block with purpose-built bar.

Saturday, I get out of bed with a single purpose in mind. The Melbourne Cricket Ground, or MCG, also known as the "G", is one of the most popular sporting stadia in Australia, famed for its International Cricket matches and winter "off-season" Australian Rules. Thousands come to see weekend games played here throughout the winter season. Melbourne also has another newly built world-class stadium, the Colonial, complete with sliding roof.

I get on a "city circle" tram plying the perimeter of the Melbourne CBD. As the tram turns a corner and negotiates its way south down Spring Street past Parliament House, I get off at Treasury Gardens and walk through to within sight of the MCG.

I arrive there in the midday heat and pay for the Stadium Tour and the museum—comprising the Australian Sports Hall of Fame which has sections devoted to both AFL and Cricket. We are led by a senior volunteer guide, around the stadium, starting with a huge, engraved metal board showing medal-winning Olympiads from the 1956 Melbourne Games. Inside the stadium, we walk down a corridor, passing hundreds of photographs of Australian Football League players.

The highlight of the tour for me is the invitation to visit the basement-level changing rooms where famous Melbourne teams like Essendon prepare. They are huge, and entire rooms are devoted to warm-up, or physio. We venture out into the stands, and examine the boxes for the TV commentators and coaches. Both coaches sit in the same box, divided only by a fault-line in the carpet. The floodlights are colossal, and the guide comments on the numbers of bulbs and prices of each. From the middle of the south stand, we can see the south-west stand is being rebuilt and lies in ruins with diggers and construction workers busy.

The Australian Cricket Board Headquarters is located here, and we make a brief and hushed, reverent tour of the small museum which contains the famous ball used in the first Ashes test.

There's an entire section devoted to the infamous 1932 "Bodyline" tour when English bowlers lobbed high "bouncers" at Australian cricketers calculated to break their nerve. (The ball bounces high into the face of the batsman, forcing him to hook the shot into the waiting hands of the fielders who have been standing close by to take the catch.)

We pause briefly outside the Members' bar, and watch well-dressed Members come and go. The waiting list is long, and it's not unusual for hopefuls to wait 25 years for a membership.

The gift shop has a well-positioned TV showing the fourth day of the action from Adelaide, with England on the brink of final collapse—in the end, Australia win by an innings and 51 runs.

An Englishman from Buckinghamshire strolls with me as we wend our way between the National Tennis Centre and International Sports and Entertainment Centre, to the Yarra River and follow it towards the main street running south-west north-east, called Flinder's Street. Here, there is a popular pub called Young and Jackson. As we are wilting in the heat, brows awash with sweat, we welcome ice-cold beer served in pint glasses.

English pints. It's like being at home back in London, only you'd think twice about ordering the half. We enjoy several and get chatting to Australian blokes at the bar.

So, I stagger back tipsy to the hostel and a quick nap there turns in to a long sleep, which is a mistake, as I had planned to catch the England-South Africa game live from Twickenham, the final Autumn International being screened around midnight.

I get up and find I've only missed the start. Die-hard rugby fans watch the action on one small TV, whilst the majority choose to watch the action from the English Premiership on the big screens. England win, thus making it three from three in the Autumn Internationals and a clean-sweep against all Tri-Nations teams, boding well for the 2003 World cup.

I walk with backpackers south down Elizabeth Street and through the Flinders Street railway station out on to the banks of the Yarra River. Crossing the river on the Princes Bridge towards the Arts Centre, we stop to look back. We can see the skyline and lights of downtown Melbourne basking under the healthy glow of a starry night. The whole effect is somewhat North American, and for an instant, it is all too easy to forget we are standing on one of the driest continents on Earth.

We walk along the embankment "Southbank" until we arrive opposite the Crown Casino. It's what you would expect of the largest in the southern hemisphere—bright, glitzy and busy. It opened in the 1990s as part of an entire rejuvenation and water-side development by the then Labour state government. Melbourne was a quieter town then, but the casino brings in interstate tourism.

I shout a round of drinks at one of the bars, and somewhat sheepishly, ask for three "cock-sucking cowboys"— the backpacker's preference.

STEPHEN MALINS

CHAPTER 17 BACK EAST

The weather turns for the worse in Melbourne, and we have a week of grey skies and drizzle. After months of washing shorts and t-shirts, I now launder jeans and thicker shirts. The effect of the weather is oppressive; I am transported back to the UK. Melbourne may as well be Birmingham now.

There is, however, the promise of a fun-packed Monday evening "Meet the Neighbours" night, where we will get a chance to meet real stars from the *Neighbours* tv show, a fixture of my childhood. People join me from the hostel to head down to Saint Kilda, in a tatty old bus, which looks like it has seen better days, with seat coverings peeling, and a pervasive mustiness.

We head past the Grand Prix track to Melbourne's seedy and fashionable beach suburb to find ourselves deposited in a queue outside a pub called the Elephant and Wheelbarrow. This is immensely popular with English backpackers, and after we are relieved of thirty dollars inside, we are kept waiting for an hour or so before the stars turn up.

Tonight, Mark Raffety who plays the evil Doctor Darcy Tyler will turn up with "Michelle Scully". They make a grand entrance to the tune from *Neighbours*, and host a round of games and a pub quiz. The characters ply the pub, and everyone gets an opportunity to have their photo taken with their chosen star, and I receive two—two!—kisses from 16-year old Kate Keltie who plays Michelle.

Saint Kilda has a reputation for both seediness and cosmopolitan bars, bistros and cafes, with a kind of atmosphere coming close to London's Camden Town, only set by a beach.

Laden with rucksack on my back, and daysack hanging down my chest, I stand in the correct spot for the tram to Saint Kilda, spending moments scurrying to and fro across the middle strip of the road trying to determine the side I need without getting cleaned out, as the trams bisect the middle of the street. After a short run, I get off not far from the beach and walk through back roads to my hostel.

The pink-coloured reception is clean, neat and tidy, but leads out to a grotty, damp, courtyard, which twists and turns around several outbuildings, with unappealing rooms tucked away in all sorts of corners. I am sharing a room with a student pilot called Richard who has been learning to fly at Moorabbin. In the late afternoon, we sit out in the courtyard and get acquainted with the local Melbourne Bitter. I am walking to one of the rank bathrooms when I bump into an Australian girl who has had a bit to drink, and is careening all over the corridor.

"Can you say I live here?" she asks.

"OK," I say.

I look up in time to see the hostel security guard coming up the corridor looking to validate her identity.

"Thanks," she says.

She comes over to myself and Richard with a friend of hers, and we head down to the Wheelbarrow pub.

On Friday, the first day of the Third test from Perth is being shown on the bar TV, and a few blokes have gathered to see how England will fare. I watch the first session. By the close of play, England are all out for 185, with Australia having amassed 126 for 2. I feel flat and completely restless in Melbourne, the grotty weather is tiresome. I'm looking forward to catching up with Dave again when he arrives.

I catch the overnight bus from Melbourne to Sydney, anticipating the arrival of better weather to come. In the interests of time, we take the Hume Highway up the guts of Victoria, sort of taking a straight line, not taking the rather more scenic Princes Highway which winds along the coast to the south. I get talking to the bus driver, who is happy to have a yarn about his work. Normally a train driver, he is driving coaches to supplement his income. He is an engaging fellow and talks to me about his life. Nearing Albury, the Victorian town near the State border with New South Wales, he explains that his wife and children live in a cottage we are about to pass on the highway (he honks his horn as we run past).

Not long after, we stop at a rest stop at Glenrowan, in the middle of Ned Kelly Bushranger territory—and most of us file off the bus into the cool night. I stand in the queue behind two Victorian police officers dressed in starched light-blue uniforms.

Looking out across the highway, I can see shadowy mountains in the distance. The resorts of Hotham and Falls Creek are not so far away—where in winter up to September, downhill skiers enjoy the short seasons in the Victorian Alps. I am standing on one of the largest, flattest continents, but a Dividing Range —a spine of hills and peaks—stretches from Queensland to Victoria, topping out at Mount Kosciuszko, some 2000 metres high—that's twice the height of Mount Snowdon, in England and Wales. Weather systems bring snow down to about 1800m on the more ambitious peaks here in Victoria, and on the "Main Range" in New South Wales, where tropical moist air from the East coast arrives and falls as snow.

Snowsport aficionados know that conditions are wet and marginal, often icy in the afternoons, it's not the powder of the US West Coast or even Japan. There's an avalanche risk—in 1997, Thredbo resort in NSW suffered a catastrophic landslide and 18 lives were lost.

The new day is only hours old when we approach Sydney from the north. From here, we get an amazing view of the Sydney Harbour bridge and CBD on the south shore. I get my first glimpse of the bridge, harbour, and the high rises, and, as always, I get a sense of excitement. Nine times out of ten, it is also a beautiful morning; does any other city in the world has this effect on me?

**

Dave spots me as he walks in through the gate of the hostel on Coogee Bay Road.

"Alright, Steve?" he asks, grinning broadly.

"Good mate," I say.

"OK," I say, "let's stroll over to the CBH and have a drink."

Dave, looking tanned and fit, but with rather sunburnt legs, is standing outside the Wizard of Oz hostel in Coogee Bay Road, beaming at me. He has just got in from Thailand. I haven't seen him for almost a year. Catching up with the details of Dave's journey, we head over to the Coogee Beach Hotel, and order schooners. We sit at the window, and look out into the bright summer's sun, watching the tourists and backpackers stroll past, reminding me of the time when I first arrived in Sydney.

Summer arrived a week ago in Sydney, with the first day of December. This means we can expect the weather to get hotter in the run up to Christmas and beyond. I catch up with all the news from home. Dave wants to head west to Perth, and as I want to travel on from there up the coast, we decide to head back there after the weekend in Sydney. Dave is feeling hungry, so I fish out pizza vouchers that have been sitting in my wallet for months, and we sit on the bench outside Dominos.

As Dave is a fit bloke, we get up early his first days and run to Bondi and back with our backpacks, and occasionally mix it up with an icy swim in Clovelly Bay. Afterwards, we do strength-building exercises outside on the hostel veranda, finishing with stretching. We are back in the room, and greet our fellow roomers, who are still fast asleep.

I promise Dave a good first days in Coogee as I had enjoyed my first weeks there. One night, an English bloke occupying the bed below him brings back a girl at about 2am in the morning. We are awoken by them coming in, as the light from outside in the corridor floods into the room. She quietly and nimbly undresses and climbs under the duvet, and he does the same and gets in with her. It's pretty obvious what's going to happen next. Soon we hear sounds of the creaking bed, and the occasional sigh of pleasure. Apart from that, they are absurdly quiet. I need to go, so when the girl gets out of bed, I get up, and open the dorm door, causing a huge flood of light to enter the room. I find the girl's friends—the backup crew—outside waiting for her to emerge.

In the morning I ask Dave how he slept over breakfast. I make light about the interruption, but I can see he is fuming:

"That bloody bloke!" he cries.

Dave of course, on top, in his ringside seat, had the creaking and motion of the bed, so was kept awake.

"I couldn't sleep," he grumbles.

***

There have been serious bush fires all over the Sydney Metropolitan area, and my aunt's house in Hornsby is at risk—again—as they watched major fires approach in 1994. It was the same last year, when smoke from fires over the Christmas period made life quite difficult in the city, and thousands of families left to escape the fumes.

Hot winds from the desert fan the blazes and tinder-dry grass provide fuel. Volunteer firefighters ("firies") fight spot fires ahead of the front caused by embers "spotting" ahead carried aloft by unstable weather.

I call my Aunt to find they have packed and are ready for the knock on the door, but are safe for the time being. People clear away leaves from gutters and choose to stay with their homes until the last moment. The Central Coast is also under attack, and huge sheaves of the Hawkesbury River are on fire, so they are back-burning to control the blaze. My cousin SMSs me to tell me they are OK.

To ring the changes, and so Dave can catch up on sleep, we move over to King's Cross, and stay in a small hostel in one of the back streets. It's a popular first-night destination for travellers, but it's impossible to walk down the main road without being accosted by men outside strip joints enticing blokes to enter their establishments. We have an Indian curry—the first I've had in months, and we chat in a local pub there.

We stroll around Darling Harbour and catch the ferry over to Watson's Bay, to visit a fish restaurant there as Dave wants to investigate a seaplane operation flying from a jetty alongside the dining room. We watch planes arrive and land in the Harbour—a party of people traipse out on to the jetty and embark somewhat nervously for a joy-flight. The plane begins its takeoff run, and at an alarmingly slow speed, labours into the sky.

Dave talks with the pilot who tells him he can pick up a seaplane rating for his Private Pilot's Licence in several hours, it's three-hundred dollars an hour for the conversion. The pilot is keen to talk and says seaplane-flying differs from normal flying.

"You don't pull back for takeoff–you allow the plane to build speed and get airborne all by itself," he says. Dave nods sagely.

***

On Tuesday the following week, Dave and I board the Indian Pacific, myself somewhat jaded, but Dave wants to fly on the West Coast. We plan to cross the continent with one stop for three days in Kalgoorlie. The journey is unremarkable, the usual endless passing of scenery by the windows. Card games of "shit-head" go a little way to relieving the monotony.

After not seeing much of half a bottle of white wine costing 12 dollars, at the stop in Adelaide, Dave and I walk from the station to a local bottle shop and buy a five-litre cask of dry white wine. We've got time to go into Burger King next door and wolf down a meal, before rushing our cask back to the station and smuggling it on board in the brief time we have allotted to us. We must cross the railway line, so to speed things up, we vault the fence and walk the embankment to the line.

In Kalgoorlie, we chuck our gear down in our room, and I am greeted by a bloke stretched out on one of the bottom bunks. I'm not sure I recognise him, and look at him quizzically.

"Over the road?" he says, and then it dawns on me. He was the young fella I met in the brothel over the road six weeks ago.

"So, how'd you go?" I ask referring to his work.

"Good mate, I had the full hour–spent a fortune," he replies, grinning. "Went off with the dark-haired girl."

We both get odd jobs. I get a day's work at a bauxite refinery and processing plant, an hour's drive out in the bush, where we spend an hour just taking a site safety and orientation course. We spend the day at height on a gantry in the middle of the plant, relining two huge pressure chambers, manhandling rubber inserts in to the hot chambers, taking it in turns to rest under what little shade we can find. It's thirsty work, but our South African supervisor looks after us. The entire plant is enclosed by a mesh fence with health and safety signage. All we are missing is watchtowers and guard dogs.

Whilst I wait for Dave to get back, I bump into an English girl in the hostel, who is selling an old backpack. We get chatting for bit, and she tells me she works as a skimpy in a bar at the very end of Hannan Street. Intrigued with her beauty and charm, and with nothing to do until Dave finishes, I decide to visit her at the pub she described. I can see there are two skimpies on shift, and I barely recognise her in her g-string. She smiles and says "Hello". We chat on and off : I give her a tip and she comes back with her address on a beer mat.

I stroll down the road back to the hostel, a little tipsy. Soon it is time to leave for the train, and Dave and I take leave of Kal, and head towards Perth.

CHAPTER 18 PILOTS IN
COMMAND – WILD WEST

We spend our first nights in Perth at Rainbow Lodge, a backpackers around the corner from the Perth interstate East Terminal, arriving just over a week before Christmas. The hostel is run by an eccentric Canadian, who employs Dave as a cook at the evening bar-b-que. He spends a few hours preparing the salads and the side dishes, and I help by taking a turn with the cooking.

Dave wants to fly the coast, from Perth to Alice Springs in the Northern Territory, following the north-west Australian coastline via Darwin.

His plan is to hire an aircraft to fly part of the distance and log flying time; accruing the "P1" or "Pilot-In-Command" hours he needs to go on and complete a Commercial Pilot's licence.

We could hire in Perth and fly north, but looking at a map, and at the huge distances between the towns, we realise this would be an expensive undertaking. Flying from Darwin to Alice would be an option, but then we would have to make a return trip to hand back the plane.

We consider hiring a car and have a trick up our sleeves. A car hire company offers a "relocation" deal free of charge if we get there in time, and pay for the fuel. We advertise for additional passengers, placing an advert in a Northbridge internet café:

Lift offered from Perth to Darwin leaving 18th December 2002

2 laid-back guys travelling by relocation vehicle. Looking for 2 passengers to share driving, fuel and fun

Pinning it on the board, we notice another one:

Wanted. Passengers interested in flying from
Perth on trips. Contact Pilot.

We see a mobile listed. As I'm out of credit, we go to the public phone in the shopping mall. Dave is soon talking to Nick, a trainee at nearby Jandakot airport, who is about to get his Private Pilot's licence. A tall and slightly chubby bloke walking by, stops, listening in to the call. He says:

"Hello mate. I'm one of the pilots who placed the advert, I'm Rich. That was Nick you were talking to."

I also get a call from our first enquirer, a girl called Georgina, around the corner, who wants to drive with us.

Over a latte, we try to marry up the goals of driving and flying. The boys talk flying, and I talk driving with Georgina. She is Polish, in her early thirties. She leaves a contact number should we decide to leave as planned.

Rich is 22, with a rotundness indicative of good living, has just graduated from a UK university.

"Myself and my mate Colin met Nick during pilot training."

Colin arrives in a Suzuki 4x4. He is slimly built, a quieter guy.

Nick is preparing for his final flight test, but we can drive to the aerodrome and wait.

"Who fancies a drink at the bar?" says Rich.

Nick turns up wearing Ray-Bans looking pleased. He's at Minovation flight school, flying Piper Warriors. He is in his late thirties, with a shock of blonde hair, and sturdily built, and a token gesture to a goatee beard. An Englishman from Hampshire, he lives in Grenoble, France, where he works as an IT contractor.

He suggests we head into town and have a Chinese meal in a restaurant he knows. Over dishes of sizzling chicken, duck, and bowls of rice, the plan takes further shape. We will be five in total, six if Georgina joins.

As soon as Nick gets his licence, and Dave has been checked out to fly, we will hire two planes. For Rich or Dave, we'll get a Cessna 172 from the Royal Aeroclub further down the apron as they have cheaper rates. Walking back to the car, Nick stops and addresses a few girls:

"Would you like to come flying with us?" They laugh, and the rest of us have a snigger at his brazen method of approach. Nick's a strong character.

It sounds great, and I would like to be a part of it. Will Georgina throw her hat in with us?

***

The next morning, we drive to the station to pick Georgina up, and she is standing on the corner with her pack ready to go. I offer her the superior opportunity to come flying with us. I point out the offer to drive with her to Darwin or Alice still stands. She accepts. We meet up with Nick in the Royal Aeroclub restaurant bar. He oozes charm involving Georgina in our ideas, and makes her feel welcome to the gang. Now we are six in total—we needed two planes.

Nick rubs his hands together and shows us a map.

"This is my plan. How about we fly to Busselton and dive the wreck of HMAS Swan there?"

We look at his WAC (World Aeronautical Charts) map of Western Australia.

"Then–let's head south-west to the Margaret River vineyards."

After that, we will head south-east to Esperance on the south coast—this will complete a circuit of the south-west tip of Western Australia. From there, we will fly two long legs; one due north to Kalgoorlie, and a final back to Jandakot.

Dave needs to get "checked out", a test by an instructor, before being able to hire a plane. Rich likewise, as this is a new hire for him. After they have completed paperwork, Georgina and I watch from the club house restaurant on the first floor as they are escorted by an instructor out to their Cessna on the apron. They carry out their visual inspection, and with Dave at the controls for the first stage, I watch him taxi out to one of the runways. He applies full power, and they hurtle down the runway until he pulls away from the ground, climbing well, before disappearing out of sight on the horizon, mired by a swath of smoke caused by a bush fire burning a few miles south of the aerodrome perimeter.

There's time to luxuriate over two flat whites before they return, and whilst Rich passed, Dave is fuming, as he made mistakes, and has therefore not got the nod today. He needs another sortie.

"It's the bloody radio that let me down," he says.

He is not familiar with Australian accents on the radio and has to work overtime to hear what is going on.

Georgina wants to buy a car, so we head west to Northbridge to an auction held in a warehouse we have heard about.

At the auction, there's a mix of cars. There are BMWs, Jaguars and Saabs and as we expected, lots of cheaper Ford sedans and station wagons. A few catch my eye; a white 1989 and bronze 1990 Falcon, all in good nick, newer than the older cars that backpackers trade. Georgina wants the 1989 Falcon and asks me to bid on her behalf. Bidding starts at 1,000 dollars. I ask Georgina if she is sure, and she nods, so I raise my hand and take the bidding to 1,500 dollars. Another bidder raises the bidding to 1,600 dollars, and I turn around once more and look at Georgina.

"Going, once..."—the auctioneer looks around—"going twice..."

"Sold! To the gentleman over there," the auctioneer cries, pointing in my direction.

I think Georgina has done well—she has a car she can hustle back to a backpacker for two to three thousand dollars.

I drive as Georgina is not confident driving on the left-hand side of the road and we head back to Rich and Colin's accommodation, a small two-bed apartment set in a long row.

We get a bar-b-que going, and Dave rustles up home-made garlic bread, and I put on rice to feed six. We get cracking with the Weber outside on the back porch, Nick arriving as the food is serving up. The conversation turns to our plan once more. There's the possibility of us taking turns to do legs in the Ford, rotating with someone in a plane for the next.

As Colin wants to return the Suzuki, we follow him to the drop-off point in the CBD, and then drive him back in Georgina's motor, giving it a bit of a burn on the highway. It's all working. We arrange the sleeping arrangements thus: Georgina and Dave kip on the sofas in the living room, and I crash in the bedroom with Rich; Colin and Nick take the second room.

Tomorrow is another chance. Dave has another attempt at the check-out, and the rest of us scratch our heads with flight-planning in an office with yellowing walls.

Rich jumps on a PC and using flight-planning software, calculates fuel requirements and weights for the trip. I make a list of airfields within range of the flight path, and photocopy information such as their position and orientation so that we know where we can divert.

"Which way does that landing strip run mate?" Nick says, swivelling around on his squeaky chair.

Dave arrives in the planning room with a sassy, smiling confident pilot, relieved he has passed his check-out under her tutelage. We are all set and prepared.

***

The day of the trip dawns. For this trip, we'll leave the Ford and take the planes. We park in the car park at the Aeroclub, and Nick is there waiting. Colin and Georgina head over with him to Minovation to hire the Warrior they want. He has chosen a retractable undercarriage variant of the basic low-wing Warrior.

Dave, Rich and I are going in a Cessna Superhawk, a faster plane than the standard 172 Skyhawk as it's equipped with a constant speed propeller unit. We collect the logbook, keys and paperwork and head out on to the apron. I check the fuel tanks, which are sloshing full to the brim, and climb in back. The boys strap in, Rich taking the left-hand seat as he will be flying the first leg to Busselton.

The plan: at Busselton, we will be picked up by a scuba school and be driven out to Cape Naturaliste for a dive of the wreck Her Majesty's Australian Ship (HMAS) Swan. This ship, once in service with the Royal Australian Navy, has now been scuttled and sent to the bottom and placed for the use of recreational divers.

Rich applies full power and soon we are running once more down the runway. As he rotates, one wing tip catches a gust, and for an alarming split second, it looks like it will catch the ground. We pull away from the runway, before banking around in a climbing turn and heading south-west towards the coast.

We ascend to 2,500 feet and watch the water to our right, and Perth disappears behind us. I grab the map and track the features below as they pass beneath us, identifying them on the map. We pass several inland lakes–a series of finger shaped waterways.

After about 45 minutes, Busselton approaches, and Rich switches to the general frequency and broadcasts his intentions. With no control tower at the field, he must follow circuit joining conventions, rules applying to aircraft wishing to land; he first makes a pass over the field at 2,000 feet to see which way the wind is going. It is coming right down the runway, in the opposite direction, so he must land against it. He turns, and circuits the field, and as he reaches the downwind section of the circuit, makes another call.

"Busselton all stations, this is Cessna Bravo–Oscar–Foxtrot downwind for full stop."

We hear no reply from any other traffic in the area, so he turns around to line up, and with myself and Dave scanning for local traffic, makes his descent on final. I watch with bated breath as the grass and the tarmac of the runway come up to meet us.

If you were slightly nervous as a passenger in a car where the driver had just passed their test; it would be the same with a pilot who has just passed theirs. Rich, however, brings her in for a perfect landing, and taxis over to the aircraft tie-down points.

"Good landing, Rich," Dave says.

I jump out on to the grass. Everywhere I look there are thousands of insects, blowing everywhere. The day is hot and dry, and the grass is dry and crisp underfoot. Rich finishes up securing the aircraft to heavy concrete ballasts, and we walk over to the field's club building. Inside, in the air-conditioning, we are greeted by a young woman in her early twenties, who in a back office, monitors the radio net, and takes payment of landing fees.

Rich calls Nick on his mobile, and he answers at once.

"Where are you?" he asks.

"We're in Busselton," replies Rich. "We landed here fifteen minutes ago. Where are you?"

"Haven't taken off yet," replies Nick, clearly annoyed. He has been saddled with a last-minute aircraft type-questionnaire he must complete before he can hire. A man pulls up in a minibus with the name of the school we arranged the dive with. We explain the delay, and he decently tells us we can delay by an hour.

One hour later, we discover Nick has only just taken off, and he won't be here for another 45 minutes. The scuba man is visibly annoyed and makes a heated call to the school. He tells us an American is waiting to dive with us who is also being delayed, and has to return a hire car before this evening or incur another day's charge. Nick is not defeated quite so easily. Rich puts him on speaker to relay.

"Mate, I'll pay your car hire if you can wait."

The American agrees.

All is well, when we hear a single engine above us and sight the blue and white Warrior. Nick has made it.

We are whisked to the scuba dive shop in Cape Naturaliste.

There, we arrive in a throng of confused, rushed-looking tourists donning gear in a mad panic, under the watchful eyes of instructors, who are assessing people for size. What is it about diving? I've yet to see a group of divers look relaxed prior to a dive. An American is there, suited up, waiting for us and grins broadly when Nick apologises for us.

One of the instructors, a stunning, statuesque, dark-haired girl with an hour-glass figure, wearing a one-piece swimsuit, ushers us into a briefing room. A diagram of HMAS Swan pinned on a chipboard tableau is balanced against a back wall. She takes us through the dive, occasionally pointing at the diagram.

"This is where we make our first safety stop," she says, pointing to a mark made by a permanent marker on the board.

I'm captivated by her, so the information goes over my head and I'm finding it difficult following. When she finishes, there are no questions.

CHAPTER 19 A DECENT DESCENT

We head out to the shore in the back of an old bus, decorated in a style and a vintage of *Scooby Doo*. A launch is waiting for us in the shallows, and our scuba tanks and BCDs are already waiting for us, neatly hanging. We're all set. We climb in, and race at high speed towards the ship. The coxswain is an experienced boat handler who is a friendly, wise-cracking soul. Dave gets his flash gear on, and Georgina is going to snorkel.

I am first in the water, executing a backwards roll and inflating my BCD. The sea has a fair bit of swell. I hold on tight to the rope being lifted against the boat with the swell. We descend slowly as a group down to about ten metres, and there we wait. Looking around, it is too dark to see the wreck below at this point but looking up the line I am reminded of the DVD box cover of *The Abyss*. Everyone is languidly hanging in the water, one arm on the descent line, strung out every five metres or so. Only the bubbles from our rigs disturb the quiet. It is very eerie.

We descend to 15 metres where we arrive on the bow of the destroyer, covered with sludge and barnacles. We are led slowly towards the stern, descending to about 24. Soon we arrive at an open hatch where we can swim through the superstructure. Our dive leader points inside, and I am first through, swimming into the gloom. In front of me, I can spy my exit, and I head straight for it, as I am not a massive fan of "overhead" diving. On the other side, we follow a walkway along the edge. I use the old steel wire fence as an aid for propulsion and receive a cut for my troubles.

We enter another hatch, but this time, the exit is upwards, towards an opening through what might have been a weapons silo. It is dark inside, but we swim towards a light where the opening is. We filter near the bridge of the destroyer, and spend time swimming around on the foredeck, watching the wildlife. Tiny fish make their homes inside little pipes, with just their faces showing. They are no bigger than a man's finger.

There's a safety stop at ten and five metres, and then we slowly ascend to the surface, hauling ourselves up the line. The sea swell has increased, and Dave helps us out by dragging the line in towards the boat. I take off my weight belt and pass it up, before climbing in.

The ride back to the shore is fast, and chilly. We all huddle in the launch as the bow rhythmically is buffeted by oncoming waves, and by wind which is picking up, rifling through our sodden hair.

With the help of the dive shop, we find accommodation at a camp site in Busselton, not far from the main street and promenade. We're sharing a cabin with five bunk beds, and a double. Georgina takes the double. We spend the evening in a bar overlooking the sea, on the promenade.

***

A taxi drops us back at the aerodrome and we are relieved to find the aircraft still firmly secured where we left them. However, another factor soon becomes apparent. To our dismay, we see the wind has not only picked up, but that it is blowing right across the runway. The windsock at the side of the runway is streaming directly towards us.

"15 knots is the maximum gents," reminds Nick.

The wind exceeds this. There is no other runway we can use. A highly skilled pilot might take off, but we, newly qualified or with little experience, dare not.

"Let's check the AFOR," Rich says.

The Area Forecast suggests the weather won't improve any time soon. We talk to pilots and staff in the club house, and they are also hanging around waiting. The girl manning the desk is still there, and says her boyfriend is out there, due in.

"We were supposed to be heading out for breakfast," she looks peeved.

We're going nowhere.

We need to go to Plan "B". There are other things we can do in this South West tip of WA. We planned to take off from Busselton, and head for Margaret River, fifteen minutes flying time, famous for the vineyards in the area, and thence to Albany. We can still do this of course. We'll hire a people carrier, and drive to the Margaret River. I'm given a lift to town and pick up an old Toyota people carrier from a garage there and get back to the aerodrome to collect the rest of the crew.

They pile in, and I take the wheel, finding the highway to Cape Naturaliste. On arriving in the Margaret River region, full of English-style winding ditch-lined roads through trees, we see signs to vineyards.

We find a chocolate factory, which has become a success story in the region since opening a few years ago, enjoying good publicity in several state magazines and newspapers. The main shop has an artisanal wood floor, with a coffee bar to one side. There are samples of chocolate under a glass presentation canopy with gourmet bars on racks. On the counter are bowls of chocolate, and using scoops, we shovel mouthfuls of plain, dark chocolate into our mouths, before re-joining the back of the queue, and going around again. At a back window, we can spot a factory worker churning a chocolate mix. He's not helping himself—but then, when you work with chocolate all day, you wouldn't want to eat it, would you?

In the car park, I don't pull away until I've policed seatbelts. This close to Christmas, Australia is operating its usual public holiday double-demerit policy, whereby driving offences carry six-point fines rather than the usual three. Only two of my passengers need to fail to fasten seat-belts, and I lose my hard-earned Western Australian driving licence.

We're on a roll, because as we continue down the road in high spirits, we come on a cheese factory—too good an opportunity to miss. We head straight for the cheese counter, where cheddar, and local specialities are on offer. Yoghurt too.

Feeling ever better, we see another sign pointing to a fudge-factory. We try not to laugh too hard when Nick asks the girl on the cash register if we can see the "fudge packers". Predictable.

We spend the night in Margaret River, at a local YHA. Before going out, we all organise the bills we have picked up for each other, trying to calculate who owes who but it disintegrates into a real farce. Rich and Nick start arguing over the best mathematical model to use—they can't agree. It's quite funny.

"So, I paid for the plane, the first day's fuel, yeah, you paid for the accommodation?" clarifies Nick.

"I get that, but I've put in for the unit–right, it all nets off mate," argues Rich. "I've taken that into account bud."

"Start again, I paid $250..." insists Nick "Your bit is 1/6th..."

Dave and I keep out, contributing only when it is time to put our hands in our pockets.

Once again, we drive back to the aerodrome, only to find the wind coming from the same direction, and speed, as before. A pilot grins.

"You should have been here first thing. The wind was right down the runway. I was up there flying." We groan collectively at our tardiness. Nick and Rich are so keen to fly, they pace out, into the wind, the distance along a strip of taxiway towards a clump of trees.

"What do you reckon, Nick?"

"10–20–30 ..." he counts, through his teeth.

If long enough, they could attempt their takeoff roll here. But whilst under perfect conditions, the length is ok—just, the trees at the end are a risk; can we can climb fast enough to gain height to clear them?

"Obstacle clearance," mutters Rich.

The whole flying trip is now a write off, as Nick needs to get back to Perth to fly home to the UK for Christmas, and none of us has time to complete the route. We must get airborne by tomorrow morning. If need be, we will bus it to Perth, and pay a fee for the club to come and pick up the aircraft—there's always a way.

We drive off once more to Cape Naturaliste, and go out to a lighthouse on the head. The lighthouse is surrounded by high grass and bush; the flies there unbearable and we are ambushed stepping outside the people carrier. The flies' natural predator, the dung beetle, has not eaten enough fly eggs, and this year the fly population is unusually high.

We walk the path to the lighthouse and back and flies swarm around us constantly, so we take cover in the tourist shop serving the lighthouse. Nick turns up wearing a mosquito net, which he is wearing beekeeper fashion, paired with a brimmed hat. We make a run for the vehicle, and closing all the windows, there is rhythmic swatting as my passengers systematically set out to rid the people carrier of flies.

***

Dunsborough is a tidy beach town on the way back to Busselton, and we spend the afternoon on the beach, not far from a campsite and we park up in the reception area and Nick uses his nascent charm to negotiate with the owners. We end with a very smart chalet, complete with video and TV, small kitchen and several bedrooms. We present Georgina with the master bedroom, and the rest of us take bunk beds in the second bedroom or the living room.

Supper is in an English-style pub outside the campsite entrance, where hundreds of people have flocked to eat, drink and dance this weekend. The beer garden has an amphitheatre style sunken lawn, full of people; and a stage and beer wagon have been set up. We have fish and chips, and bump into the scuba instructors from the day before. Colin enters a raffle and wins a prize—an old surfboard belonging to a famous surfer. He gets offers from other Australians there. (The highest is 300 dollars.)

Nick and I circulate the crowds, chatting. He plies his charm, and I act as his wingman, following him with amusement as he works the crowd, striking up random conversations. If the subject is female, most of these conversation topics are steered around to flying. I get talking to a Queensland country girl, who is small and wild looking; chatting to her, you get the impression everything goes. She asks me about a lift to a party, but the others have just left to go for a midnight swim. Despite my drunkenness, we flirt some more. Nick has had less success, but we go back to their beach chalets and sit outside under the stars, talking to our new friends.

Driving back to Busselton, Rich and Nick have a massive row. There's been tension between them. Nick seems to operate in his own time zone and likes things his own way—it's his way or the highway. He emphatically debates every point to the nth degree, so group decisions take a long time. In his favour, though, he is excruciatingly fair about everything. So—he is annoyed he has paid a lot of money for firstly his pilot's licence, and secondly, the Warrior with the retractable undercarriage, yet is not going to get much money back, as he can't charge anyone for a trip we weren't able to complete.

Nick wants to put a vote to the group to reimburse him. Rich, disagreeing with his argument, sabotages and shakes his head.

"I want the group to decide, Rich!" shouts Nick.

He is practically on top of Rich, in a rage. It seems to me the combined egos of pilots and a trainee in one people carrier, not able to fly is causing a lot of tension. Dave and I keep out of it.

At the aerodrome, the wind has dropped, and we think we can take off. Too big for the back of a Cessna, Colin leaves the surfboard in the aerodrome's office. Nick and Dave are pilots for the next leg. Nick, Georgina and I jump in the Warrior. It's a low-wing design, and I am impressed with the light and space in the cockpit, and the visibility all round. In the Cessna, the cockpit is dark—the Warrior seems like a real plane, not a box with wings mounted on top.

We watch the others take off first in the Cessna, and we follow.

They have a ten-minute lead on us, but the Warrior is faster with its retractable undercarriage, and after twenty minutes flying, we hope to gain a visual sighting. Nick gets nervous that we will run in to them, and looks around, performing long, slow banks so he can see below the wings.

"Can you see them, guys?"

We're all eyes in the back.

We establish radio contact with Dave, but we still cannot see them. After scanning the horizon, we hear Dave squawk on the radio.

"You're about half a kilometre off to our right!"

Sure enough, we can see them out to sea, to our left. We close the distance.

Back at Perth, Nick performs a fantastic straight-in landing, and we taxi over to Minovation. Traipsing through the school, I spot tens of past successful students commemorated by lines of photographs mounted on the wall. My eye strays and focuses on a single photo in the lines—recognising the name underneath:

Daniel Watkins - PPL November 2001

I am amused but not surprised to have singled out this photo, as this was my ex-girlfriend's supervisor, who left for Australia several years ago chasing his dreams. It seems our lives ended up intersecting in some ways.

The others join us, having landed not long after. Colin realises he has left his mobile on-charge back in Busselton, but he needs to recover the surfboard anyway, so jumps in the Ford and heads back down south. Nick busies himself with packing as he needs to catch a flight back to the UK. Time to renegotiate accommodation for the rest of us at Nick's now vacant chalet.

Nick has asked us to drive him over to Perth International, and we wave him a cheery goodbye. On the way back, we receive a phone call from Rich who sounds very stressed, demanding we come and pick him up as he is in a bit of a stew. He tells us the manager of the chalet accommodation got so angry, he started throwing around Rich's gear. Intrigued, we assume he had been rude, so we go around there ourselves to find a polite and well-meaning man. He explains the price tariff, which we clarify. Then the man turns on us, and gets visibly annoyed.

"Are you blokes stupid!? F**ck off! I've had enough."Dave and I turn on our heels. Rich is right, he's a character. Thus, having drawn a blank at airport-based accommodation, we load the car and drive over to East Perth, back to Rainbow Lodge.

Colin arrives late that night, after a gruelling six-hour round trip. The surfboard is lying on the backseat. I hope it was worth it.

CHAPTER 20 ROADS AND ROADHOUSES - THROUGH WA AND THE KIMBERLEYS

Flying and Driving Day 1: Christmas Eve Perth – Kalbarri

Georgina and I have decided to go through with our plan to drive from Perth to Alice Springs in her Ford. I am looking forward to it, as I fancy the open road. To trek along the highways is to discover an ever-unwinding scenery punctuated, yes, by lonely roadhouses. I once drove from LA to Vegas, on to the Grand Canyon—thence San Francisco in a few weeks. The open road is liberating. Rich, Dave and Colin won't join us as they want to log more flying hours for their budding careers.

Zero hour is Christmas Eve. I am going to drive the first leg to Geraldton, a 250-mile trip, mostly along the North West Highway. We fill the Ford's tank up at the servo opposite the hostel and Georgina pays for the fuel.

It is straightforward heading out of the city, and we drive through the Perth city traffic, finding the route to Highway One to connect with the north-bound North Coastal Highway. As the Perth suburbs give way to country lanes and bush, I have a crisis of confidence, and after pulling over at a farmhouse selling eggs and veggies, and a brief chat with the landowner there, find I am indeed on the right route.

Driving north we find the countryside becomes dryer and dryer, and the traffic thins out appreciably. The terrain is similar to the bush I saw out in Leonara when we were drilling, but the trees are taller, thicker, and closer to the road, making it difficult to see far off the road. The soil is a deep red. The only vehicles we see are road-trains, and utes all heading south towards Perth for

Christmas.

Geraldton is a large town (by Western Australia standards): mini-malls, shops, a bottle shop and new estates.

As Georgina prepares to drive for the first time, my phone bleeps, and I get an SMS from Dave.

"Steve–we're around the corner mate."

The boys have just landed at Geraldton aerodrome, five kilometres away. They could be leaving very soon, so Georgina and I turn around. As this is her first time behind the wheel, and she is not used to driving on the left, she cuts across the road on the wrong side. I had promised not to "shout at her", but there is a subdued agony in my voice. Making another turn, she turns on the wipers rather than the indicators.

"It's OK Georgie! Don't worry," I say.

Pulling up in the aerodrome car park overlooking the apron, I recognise the Cessna from the tail-plane markings, and we greet them like we've haven't seen them for years. They've just hopped over from Perth, whereas it has taken us a good six hours! We explain we are heading to Kalbarri, a coastal beach area in a protected national park, a two-hour scenic drive from here, and so they plan to meet us there with the plane for Christmas night. I have a brain wave; as our flying excursion was cut short, I might as well get a chance to fly as a passenger on this next leg, and so I switch places with Colin, and he gets in the Falcon. Without delay, he drives off with Georgina towards Kalbarri.

Rich unhitches the line from the av-gas fuel tank bowser and refuels the plane, paying with his Aeroclub Esso card. Dave climbs in the left-hand seat and assumes Pilot in Command. We taxi to the runway. As the wind was crosswind on arrival, they landed on a poorly maintained runway on 05. Now we can take off from the main runway, and Dave executes a nice take off roll, and climbs away from the field.

With no control tower, they are not sure what the procedures are for departing the field and begin to debate it. I call out from the back seat:

"How about ascending to 1500 feet and then waiting until you are three nautical miles from the airfield."

I'm not sure if I am right here, but Rich looks around and says,

"What was that Steve?"

I repeat my suggestion.

Rich looks at Dave, nods and says,

"That's sounds about right." He looks back at me.

"Steve. I'm glad you're here."

Further uncertainties and dramas await us. Heading towards Kalbarri is simply a matter of following the coastline north, but we can see a thick bank of low-level cloud reaching out in front of us. Dave heads for a small gap he can see. Rich clutches Dave's arm:

"No!–Don't fly through cloud. We're not allowed to!" cries Rich.

Dave says he can manage, and the pair have a heated discussion. We could fly out to sea, where there is less cloud, but this is not a good idea. We have no idea what the cloud cover is like above the aerodrome in Kalbarri, and if we cannot see the field, we should consider aborting the flight and returning.

He flies an orbit whilst they consider their options. The problem is that he has had a fair bit of experience in flying through broken cloud as he flies routinely in the UK, whereas Rich has less confidence spoilt by perfect Western Australian conditions.

We are at about 800 feet, trying to find a way through. I make myself useful, and look around us for traffic, and keep an eye for the ground. We have been circling houses and farms for a while, and I watch them spiral below. I glance over at the altimeter and notice we have lost a fair bit of height—and I am alarmed to see the altimeter unwind lazily. Watching it unnerves me.

"Watch your height mate!" I warn. Rich is now getting nervous and checks our height. I get a feeling of unease and hope they can cope.e

We need to locate the landmarks that will bring us back to the field at Geraldton. We're not sure exactly where we are, and there is nerves whilst we scan for them.

It's a relief to see the industrial towers that mark the edge of the perimeter, and Dave skirts them, before turning on his downwind leg. He's a bit low in the circuit as he maintains his height below the cloud at about 600 feet. He executes a nice landing, and as we roll to a full stop, Dave mutters, shaking his head,

"I feel much better about my landings now."

We get out and head over to the terminal, beaten again by the elements. An hour has elapsed, and Georgina and Colin will be halfway to Kalbarri now in what might have been the choice of transport. We are not excited by the idea of spending Christmas night in Geraldton.

In the terminal, at the car hire kiosk, we place a call to the Avis rep, only to discover Christmas call-out rates apply. Fortunately, the rep takes pity on us and by giving us all the concessionary rates, can rent us a Holden Commodore at a reasonable rate between the three of us. She arrives from home—it is after all, Christmas Eve, and gives us the keys.

"Now boys, you take care of driving in the dusk on those roads up to Kalbarri. There's plenty of kangaroos about."

She's right: it will be dark in another two hours.

"OK. When you return the car, just lock the keys in the boot as we won't be here. OK?"

We find the Commodore out in the car park, a brand-new red 4 litre V6. Rich takes the wheel.

The country changes to winding roads through beautiful, vibrant crops and fertile plains. The sun is low in the sky heralding the end of the day. No sign of roos. It is dark when we get to Kalbarri and we can see the sea but little of the surrounding countryside.

Colin and Georgina got a room for our group, complete with ensuite shower and toilet. After a drive around, invigorated and fresh from a swim, we have dinner in a steakhouse restaurant which is still doing food. I order steak and chips, Colin has the scotch fillet. We wash all the food down with a bottle of wine, and glasses of beer, and play cards and drinking games out on the terrace.

Christmas Day

We sleep in. Looking outside, I can see Kalbarri is on one side of an inlet. It's beautiful. I start singing "Good King Wenceslas", and "Ding-Dong Merrily on High" at the top of my voice, and jump in the shower, feeling great.

Time for that Australian Christmas Day tradition—a drive down to the beach. We spend an hour there, shared only with one other family, and stray walkers. It is over 30 degrees, and the sand is hot. Dave joins me in a quick run up and down the beach, the soles of our feet burning up if we dally too long in any one place.

In the hostel, and in high spirits, we sit at a covered area full of tables with about 30 backpackers. The staff have laid on Christmas lunch for us, with bowls of salad, cold cuts, and fruit. In a fridge, next to the bar-b-que, there are tinnies of beer and coke, and there are casks of red and white wine out on the tables for people to help themselves. The only condition of entry is "wear a hat" and "pull a cracker". After the main course, it is time for the games.

The hostel owner, a bearded Australian in his fifties, suspends a balloon *pinata* covered in papier-mâché, from one of the beams supporting the covered area, and invites blindfolded residents to come forward. I volunteer first, and I am guided to a position within striking distance. I raise the stick slowly in front of me, judge the distance, and attack the balloon. After more guys have whacked it around, a bloke is able to cut it in half with a single swipe.

The owner comes around, and we discover he is a pilot and he tells us of the times he has flown at ridiculously low levels to get back to Kalbarri when the weather has closed in. His friends have come to help, and they bring out a flaming Christmas pudding before retiring out to the lawns to play cards.

Boxing Day

Georgina and I go out to the coast with locals who are keen abalone fishermen. We follow their Toyota out to a car park, a few kilometres out of town, overlooking the sea. One has a permit which allows him to hunt the rock pools of the coastline. We follow a path down through dunes, and then cross a rocky bowl down to a cliff with views over a sheltered system of coves and inlets. The water is turbulent here, with white horses on the crests. The boys gingerly make their way down to the sea, and dive in. Inside twenty minutes, they are back with about ten lobsters—and tens of abalone.

Back at the hostel, the fishermen pour their catch in to two huge pans on the communal stove out in the courtyard and the owner comes out and lays the table.

The Boxing Day Test is being broadcast from the MCG, and Australia have won the toss and elected to bat first. The opening Australian partnership gets to 195, before the loss of the first wicket. (Incredibly, Jason Langer is to amass 250 runs in this Fourth Test.) The owner sits opposite me for dinner, and we talk about life in Australia over a bottle of wine. We also discover one of the fishermen has a sideline making jewellery: etched ingots from silver and gold based on customer designs and we watch as he demonstrates his catalogue to two girls from England.

Driving Day 2: Kalbarri – Denham

We leave early towards the Shark Bay peninsula, and Monkey Mia. We arrive at the Overlander Roadhouse, refuel, and fork off the main North West Coastal highway in the direction of Denham.

We detour about three miles to Hamlin Pool, to look at stromatolites. They are a kind of "living fossil", created over thousands of years by small microbes feeding on tiny particles of carbon and calcium, swept in on the ebbing tide.

"Steve–they are literally one of the earliest forms of life on Earth," Georgina says, looking at the *Rough Guide*.

At an old telegraph station, we walk along a boardwalk that has been constructed for viewing this rare marine landscape and find we've come at the right time and the fossils are not submerged. No wonder Shark Bay is a World Heritage Area.

Another detour leads to the stunning expanses of the very aptly named Shell Beach. This 110-kilometre beach is made entirely of tiny white shells, metres deep in places. Apart from a German couple strolling holding hands, Georgina and I have the beach to ourselves. The breaking ocean is incredibly inviting so Georgina frolics in the surf in a stretchy one-piece.

Denham is Australia's western-most town and the main centre servicing the Shark Bay Marine Park. Two-thirds the way up the narrow Peron Peninsula, it is a small prawning town.

On the other side of the peninsula directly east of Denham, Monkey Mia is the small resort town on the shores of the park, famous for its playful, visiting bottle-nosed dolphins. Daily, they swim inshore to the shallow waters gently bumping against the legs of excited tourists, as they seek a free feed from the ranger. It's an opportunity to get up close and personal with these intelligent creatures.

Eco-cruises sail visitors into the otherwise unexplorable and remote sections of the Shark Bay Marine Park. The park's boundaries protect other special marine wildlife species, like sea turtles and dugongs.

Georgina and I book into a hostel with a reception block and rooms on both sides of a large pool. Two English girls from Kalbarri turn up with a group of travellers who are driving with a tour company. I get in to a conversation about Australia with them and whilst they like travelling in Australia, they are agreed on one thing; the overt sexism of Australian men and their patriarchal attitude.

"Aussie men treat you like second-class citizens. We've been wolf-whistled ever since we got here. In many ways this is a country still in the Dark Ages," says one.

I suggest perhaps this male attitude is true anywhere and would not be out of place on a building site in the UK. As I tell them, I think I can understand some of the story; to all intents and purposes Australian men, particularly bushmen have a kind of bluster; it generally seems harmless. Furthermore, Australian women seem well equipped to deal with it and have a toughness of their own. Maybe it stems from history, on sheep stations, men traditionally worked long hours in the fields, and so the women were left to manage the property; thus developing an independence.

Driving Day 3: Denham – Coral Bay

Georgina is driving before noon, setting a pattern for the rest of the trip. As we have not refuelled since the Overlander Roadhouse, she keeps an eye on the fuel gauge as we retrace our steps.

At the roadhouse, we fill up and then head north on to Carnarvon and Coral Bay, our destination for today. We drive past a banana and mango plantation, on the outskirts of town. Passing through the Carnarvon town centre, we can see nothing but a main strip of "Australia Anywhere", with a single pub of note, and a Woolworths peeking out in a little mall at the end of the road by the beach. We drive along a back road to the beach and find they are bordered by high dunes. I park the car behind an old yellow Sigma, touched by rust, near a gap in the dunes, and Georgina skips out for a swim.

Dying for a midi, I drive back down to the pub in the main street I saw and find a plum spot right outside. A skimpy leans over the bar. I get talking to her, and it turns out she is a Californian, now living in Australia.

On my return, Georgina is stretched out on her towel, drying out, hands and wrists upturned with beads of water on her hair.

We approach a large sign on the side of the road, and I slow down so we can read it. It marks the Tropic of Capricorn, and we cross it at the latitude 23 degrees south of the equator, marking our passage into the Tropics with two seasons—the "wet" and the "dry". We take photographs, as do an Italian family that pull up in a blue 4x4.

Coral Bay is a very small tourist spot, at the southern end of the Ningaloo Reef, Australia's "other reef"—260 kilometres of expanse, only less visited. The beach is beautiful and deserted. The whole town feels like it has yet to be discovered.

We check in to the brand-new hostel and find the Italian family have got there first and we wait half an hour whilst they book the entire family in and all their excursions for the following day. The father wears a salmon linen shirt and exquisite leather sandals. Are there any rooms left, I wonder?

It would be nice to get a place for the night.

For our evening entertainment, we thread our way through cheap metal tables and scattered chairs to the bar, open on one side. I get myself and Georgina a drink. A band is playing in one corner, and all tables near the bar are full, so we settle for a table outside, where an English couple joins us.

Jane has been travelling on her own, through Thailand, and her friend has come over from the UK to visit her, he's a quiet guy. Jane is a petite girl with dark hair, clever and chatty. She wears practical Birkenstocks—the ones with feet-shaped footbeds. Back in the hostel we have glasses of red from a cask Georgina and I opened for dinner.

Soon, we're all roaring drunk, and Jane's friend goes to bed, leaving me and Jane to chat. We go over to a group of Australians smoking pot, or rather scale the railings by the swimming pool, making an awful noise, and Jane grabs a spliff off someone. The pot is particularly potent, and presently, her eyes are bloodshot. We get up, and stumble over to a staircase and sit there for a bit. Then we kiss, and I tell her she is gorgeous, with her big eyes. I realise I am locked out of my room, so I jump into bed with Jane. Her friend is in the bed above us and stirs as we sneak in, so I look apologetically at him.

***

At a rude hour, the next day, with headaches, Georgina and I head out to the tour shop, and grab fins, mask and snorkel. Our guide leads out across pristine white sand to a boat, moored in the shallows.

The boat trip is advertised as a Turtle Cruise and snorkel trip and we are hoping to see Manta Rays. Some boats are in radio contact with light aircraft, poised to spot the Rays from overhead. However, the coxswain of the boat takes us out to an area where Manta Rays have been seen the day before, and the guide points out shapes feet below the surface. We look down and see black shapes swimming by the bow.

"That's a male in pursuit of a female," the coxswain says.

Next, we arrive at a turtle colony, where the water is shallow and choppy, and turquoise-coloured, fringed with coral, and all at once, we see tens of turtles, which congregate around the gunwale. Every so often, a snout or a face breaks the surface, much to the delight of the children on board.

In a popular snorkel spot, we jump into the water and enjoy the reef; I haven't snorkelled since I tried it in a swimming pool on a SCUBA course years before, and it is great kicking around the coral unencumbered. The leader takes us out to a deeper area of water between two banks of coral, where sharks have been sighted, and we swim after her with trepidation. I put my head up and see the boat is hundreds of yards away making me feel isolated but blissfully free at the same time.

At dinner, the group eats out by the swimming pool. Georgina prepares cheese and rocket salad, and we invite a truck driver to join us. He is from Sydney and is travelling. He and I go out to the bottle shop in his ute. Georgina says she wants to swim, and we watch as she runs in to the surf. It's bloody cold, and afterwards, we head out to the bar and grab drinks.

CHAPTER 21 THE TOP END

Driving Day 4: Coral Bay – Karratha

Time to leave Coral Bay. We are now near the top of Western Australia, where the coastline wheels from a due north direction to a north-east one. We start the long drive towards Broome. It's a two-day drive, punctuated by nothing but roadhouses, endless highways and the coastal towns of Port Headland and Karratha. The first roadhouse is called Minilya and we refuel here from a shuddering pump which has seen better days. The truck driver is here, in his Toyota, and when we pull forward to park, we are wing-mirror to wing-mirror to Jane's Ford—they shimmy past us with an armful of supplies.

"Guys…" her friend acknowledges.

After a few hours driving, we pull up at the Nanutarra roadhouse. We find a pleasant cafeteria, and a small garage presided over by a friendly, laid-back mechanic. We get him to look at the AC unit as there's a noise developing. He pops the bonnet. As I suspected, the problem lies with the auxiliary ac belt, not the main fan belt.

Driving is becoming a routine—I give it that. We drive at 100 km per hour to save fuel—a speed that would seem ridiculously slow in the UK, where anyone driving at less than eighty miles an hour is dawdling. But we have plenty of time on our hands, and scant people on the road to displease. The Ford's large engine is silent at this speed and is not overheating. We see the occasional ute and police car. Everyone waves hello as we drive past. Locals raise an index finger off the wheel—presumably, it's too hot to wave.

The road and verges are littered with roadkill; cows, sheep, kangaroos, and sometimes, in the heat of the afternoon, we catch a waft of the smell of rotting carcass as we speed by. The larger animals require a small detour on to the other side of the road. We stop at every roadhouse out of curiosity more than anything else, and always to have a drink and cool down.

Fortescue roadhouse sells postcards of the servo during recent severe floods.

Back on the main highway 250 kilometres north of the turnoff to Exmouth and Coral Bay, a road branches left towards the coast, ending in the town of Onslow. Once the mainland base for British nuclear experiments at the nearby Montebello Islands, the town now services the nearby offshore gas and oil rigs.

Aboriginal for "Good Country", Karratha is a newer service town established in the late 1960s to support the Pilbara's vast mineral wealth. It services a sizeable off-shore gas industry. The shopping area is huge and is reputed to be one of the largest in Western Australia outside Perth. Our hostel is tiny, but well equipped with a kitchen, TV lounge, study room and tables outside in a courtyard. There's a cinema here, showing the next instalment in *Lord of the Rings: The Two Towers.*

Driving Day 5: Karratha – Port Headland - Broome

An early departure from Karratha towards Port Headland. From Port Hedland to Broome is 400 miles, or 600 kilometres.

The landscape after Karratha is different to the stumpy tree-lined bush we have seen hitherto; it is open, flat and expansive. Rain clouds are visible. Georgina is driving in the mornings, as has become her habit. I am engrossed in *Apocalypse 2000*, a 1981 book written by Charles Berlitz about his predicted end of the world in the New Millennium. He got it wrong there.

I hear an agonised, wailing sound from Georgina:

A small kangaroo is standing on the side of the road, facing me. For a split second, the kangaroo—a young one by the look of it—is going to be ok, as it hops out of harm's way. As we get close, it hops back again, though, and there is no way we are going to miss it. I have time to see the look of bewilderment and surprise on its face before the corner of the bumper strikes it, spinning it off to the side. In detached shock, we don't think to stop to check whether it is dead or not, but I think Georgina is shaken though. She drives to lunchtime, then I take over and she gets in the back of the car, stretches out, and goes to sleep.

The Pardoo roadhouse is halfway betwixt Port Hedland and Broome, near Eighty Mile beach. The Sandfire roadhouse is on a rather run-down ramshackle plot, and we walk across cracked and peeling lino to the counter to buy a bottle of Coke. On sale on battered shelves are stubbie holders depicting the 1996 Cyclone Olivia that hit the area.

The strongest Australian cyclones have crossed Western Australia's north-west coast: the area at risk is the section of coast from Broome to Shark Bay. In December 1975, Cyclone Joan crossed the Western Australian coast—winds in Port Headland gusted to 132 miles per hour. The most famous cyclone occurred on Christmas Day, 1974, when Cyclone Tracy hit Darwin: winds gusted to 135mph taking 65 lives.

On the approach to Broome, the desert landscape changes back to a flat plain of green, lush grass, heralding the start of civilisation. Not so civilised: insects on the road get sucked up into the car. Hundreds hit the front, coating the grill and headlights, and splatter on the windscreen.

Lying in between green mangrove mudflats and the turquoise waters of the Indian Ocean, Broome's early fame derived from its world-beating pearl industry, attracting fortune-seekers in the late nineteenth century. Today, it's best known as one of the nation's true getaways, luring tourists dreaming of lazing on unspoiled white beaches in the middle of nowhere.

As to be expected of any beach mecca, the township's fabulous shores are matched by a range of swish resorts. There are also shops which showcase the town's pearling trade. The town is known for an effect "Staircase to the moon", during the full moon. It is relaxed here, and not for nothing is the town known for being on "Broome time".

To my surprise, I bump into Barry from Kalgoorlie, who is now minus the bargain ute, and I join him for a drink by the bar. Georgina and I have arrived in time for New Year's Eve, and armed with copious amounts of alcohol, we jump in minibuses provided and go down to the beach, where a band has set up on the sand. Georgina has been swimming in the sea, and she wiggles over to me and gives me a hug.

It is now very humid. The days are as hot as they could be without being unbearable; entering the pool area and crossing the concrete is to run the gauntlet as the super-heated bricks burn the soles of your feet. The rooms at night are sticky; I choose to sleep on the couch by the TV, or in a hammock by the pool.

Georgina wants to see a film at the open-air cinema. We see *Crackerjack*, an archetypal Australian comedy about a Victorian man who joins a bowling club just for the free parking passes and ends up winning the competition and saving the club from extinction.

Driving Day 6: Broome – Kununurra

We rest and relax a few days in Broome, but I am glad to get away from the perma-sterility of the resort. Georgina is once more driving the first half of the day, and so I settle in the passenger's side with Sadie Frost's first novel, 2000's *White Teeth*. It is the story of two ethnic families living in London, whose children come to meet a middle-class white family with funny consequences. It is hilarious, with witty insights into multicultural London.

We come on a lone cyclist, bent deep over his handlebars. We pull over beside the road and wait for him to catch us up. He tells us in an exhausted voice he is from Germany. He worries me, as he looks absolutely gone–he carries his head low, and his skin is flushed and red. Knowing that we are only an hour from the next roadhouse, I gave him all our water, and fruit, and he accepts them gratefully. Having made sure he is alright, we press on, shaking our heads at the ambitious task he has set himself.

Fitzroy Crossing, population 1150, is a dump, to be honest. It is situated below the Devonian Reef National Parks on the Great Northern Highway, 217 kilometres from the Derby turnoff. We met two Canadians who have been cycling around Australia in a kind of low-rise tandem, rather like those Sinclair C5s you used to see in the 1980s. It has taken them weeks to cycle the distance we have driven in a single day. They have a website with photographs, interviews, daily temperature updates and distances cycled.

Nearing Hall's Creek, we drive the southern extremities of the Kimberley's and start to ascend. The terrain has more open space and red rock formations—I am reminded of my drive through California's River of Fire National Park. The land is ideal cattle country, and this is where TV documentary makers come to film cattle drives from helicopters.

Hall's Creek is an old gold rush town. A near-vertical quartz vein protrudes impressively from a rock outcrop, to form the startling white and appropriately named China Wall. Halls Creek also acts as a distant base to the near kilometre-wide Wolfe Creek Meteorite Crater. Over 50 metres deep, this impressive site sacred to the Jaru Aboriginal people, is the second-largest crater of its kind in the world. The town, also known as "Hell's Crack", is well served by several modern-looking servos. We choose Esso.

Georgina sits down in the restaurant section of the servo, and I go over to the counter and order food and drink to take over there. I also ask whether I can have the key to the toilet. The lady disappears out back to the kitchen. She emerges not long after with tea and coffee, then disappears. Her colleague, a younger woman, comes out behind the counter, and another party arrives and asks for the key, and she gives it out. I resume my seat, then see the original lady come out of the kitchen, so get up to remind her. The second lady is frosty:

"I'm not going to give it out, and in any case, we only allow our restaurant guests to use the facilities."

"Well, I have ordered tea, coffee, and food," I say, pointing to the cup of tea I have in hand.

"No–you have to buy proper food from the restaurant menu, not just takeaway food," she snaps.

I look down at the china mug, and perhaps a trifling cheekily and wearily, reply:

"Well, if it's takeaway, then I can keep the china mug, then?"

"You can," she observes, "but I'll call the police!"

"I'm sorry?" I say amazed. "Is this the way you talk to customers?" I add. "We certainly won't be coming back."

"Well, we don't need customers like you, here," she replies tartly.

Before dark, we have travelled as far as we've ever managed on one tank, and we're not sure we have the endurance to make it to Kununurra. We pull into a tiny servo advertising helicopter flights and campsite in Turkey Creek, housing an Aboriginal reserve. Despite the repeated attempts of the young English girl from the servo to fix it, we gamble with what we have left in the tank.

"Youse take care," she calls after us.

Georgina drives, and soon it is dark. I keep my eyes peeled on the road, for any wildlife. We don't see anything, apart from a single cow illuminated in the headlights standing by a bridge.

Our arrival in Kununurra is signalled by us crossing a huge dam wall, sinister in the dark, and there are kilometres of campsites and outer suburbs to negotiate before we arrive in the town.

Kununurra, meaning "Big Water", is "new", established through the introduction of the Ord River irrigation scheme in 1963. Purnululu (Bungle Bungle) National Park is not far away.

Further to the south is Lake Argyle, the Southern Hemisphere's largest body of freshwater, containing enough water to fill 18 Sydney Harbours.

After a circuit around the town centre, Georgina and I find the hostel and call the out-of-hours number listed. The owner, dressed in shorts, a floppy hat, and a grubby t-shirt emerges. We get the keys to a room chilled to like a freezer in a bottle shop. Here is Anna, a petite Swiss-German girl, about five feet tall travelling with a travel companion she has met called Klaus, an articulate, bespectacled trainee English teacher from Germany.

"Want to join us for a canoe on the Ord River tomorrow?"

So, we launch our canoes from a jetty on the west bank and paddle out, with the girls in one canoe, and Klaus and I in the other. We have the coldbox in our canoe and waterproof barrels each for our spare clothes and cameras. We explore: the Western Australian sun watches out of azure skies. The rocks on the edge are alight with yellow, and the foliage of the trees bright green. It is staggeringly beautiful. The sun reflects off the water and gives it a unique hue of its own.

We find our first inlet, and head in and are astonished to find a beautiful backwater, full of overhanging trees, vines, submerged branches and trees, and bullrushes. Klaus loves how the sky is mirrored in the still of the water, and we enjoy simply drifting, taking pictures. After a meander of 300 metres down-river, we drag our canoes onto a bank leaving them in the shade of a tree, at a disused boat club, and spend a bit of time sunbathing and cooling off in the water. It is another hot day, and splashing around in the shallows, we seek the cold spots in the water.

It's been pointed out the entrance to a lagoon is marked by a sign. Crossing a crocodile net, we arrive to find it swamped with bull rushes that foul our canoes. The canoes are helplessly unbalanced with all the "boy muscle" in one boat, and so I swap places with Anna.

We backtrack down the river. With more power onboard, Georgina and I pull away from Klaus and Anna—we see and smell a bat colony, and the lagoon bends in several directions until it opens out.

An hour before sunset, we are enjoying the hostel swimming pool. The owner wanders over in his thongs (flip-flops) and asks if we'd like to view the sunset at the river. There's a fair bit of interest. Several miles out of town at the river, a ford is marked out by a rusty, but emphatic sign halfway. It's just under a foot deep, here, so I take off my trainers. Hobbling down to the sign, where the water gushes and babbles, we notice it says:

Warning. Saltwater (Estuarine) crocodiles are known
to inhabit this river. Proceed at your own risk

I turn around and regard the hostel owner with incredulity. He shrugs, and says without any doubt:
"The water is fast running here. Crocodiles don't like it. The locals come down here all the time."
Sure, enough, 4x4s drive slowly across the ford, and park, and parents, some with children no older than three—get out and stand on the rocks.
All the while, a watchful pair of eyes regards us from a distance. I shrug off the danger and focus on my footing.
At the relative safety of the rocks, people strip off, and a group of German girls, all blessed with goddess-like figures frolic into the pool of water. They get several yards and get knocked over in the water, such is the onslaught of the current. The best course of action is to sit on the bottom, and crab along on your hands.
The sun careens to the horizon and lights up sun-kissed, bronzed happy backpackers. We dry off and get changed on the rocks, and one of the German girls unselfconsciously whips off her bikini top to reveal a large pair of breasts with aureoles the size of two-pound coins.
We've had a physical day, so get an early night. I fight a losing battle with sleep trying to read pages from a novel. My sleep is interrupted in the early hours of the morning, when with the

air-conditioning on full blast, I awake, freezing cold.

CHAPTER 22 RED CENTRE AND
A TOWN LIKE ALICE

Driving Day 7: Kununurra - Katherine

As Anna and Klaus are also travelling to Katherine, we decide to drive in a kind of relaxed convoy, meeting up at rest stops. Klaus drives Anna in an off-white mid-1980s Ford Falcon Station Wagon with a Victorian plate.

We head down the Victoria Highway wanting to put some miles under our belt. We pass a large sign indicating the Northern Territory, which tells us to put our watches forward one and a half hours. This time difference is partly attributable to the fact the Northern Territory is on the same time as South Australia, but Western Australia observes Daylight Saving Time, and the NT doesn't. I find it strange: we haven't physically gained any distance west or east.

The Northern Territory covers about 20 percent of Australia and has about 1 percent of the population. Like parts of South Australia, it's a real lonely place. It's a Territory, and not a State (nor Jurisdiction.) The northern section of the NT is known as the Top End, and this is where a visitor can find the famous parks of Kakadu. However, parts of these will be closing now due to the onset of the wet season. This is where people reputedly go "troppo" with the high temperatures and excessive humidity, and where the only time you are cool is seconds after turning off the shower. As the locals like to say, reach for the towel too soon, and you'll break out in a sweat.

Timber Creek is our first stop. The fuel price tops my mental petrol price league table, an exorbitant $1.25 per litre. Inside, a small bar; and pride of place is the Darwin Stubby—several litres of beer.

The weather changes from the blue skies we have experienced

ever since we left Perth and the sky starts to cloud over, and it spits a little. Katherine is now 300 kilometres distant, and we see a sign for the famous Victoria River Downs station.

Katherine is a four-hour drive across the border, and we pull up at the Kookaburra Lodge: accommodation motel-style, but hostel-priced. The hostels in the quieter parts of Australia are getting better and better—yet cheaper too.

The rear offside tyre on the Ford is getting soft, so suspecting a slow puncture, we head off to a tyre-fitting service on the main street. They jack up the car, and diagnose a faulty valve, and refuse to take any money for their time or the replacement.

The large Aboriginal population doesn't go unnoticed: I nip into Woolworths, and on the way out come face- to-face with an indigenous person and he gazes at me sightlessly, clutching a beer bottle in hand. He takes a step backwards and falls over, cracking his head on the pavement. He knocks himself out cold for an instant, and then comes to, rubbing his head with his spare hand. I go to his aid, but he refuses help, so I leave him sitting grumbling to himself.

Klaus and Anna have arrived and are in the same room. I change in to running shorts and t-shirt and go for a run around the block—braving the humidity although it is cooler today.

So on to Katherine Gorge, in the Nitmiluk National Park. The gorge is several miles long and is divided into smaller canyons along its length. It has started to rain. The wet has been overdue. It is now mid-January, and we can expect the wet to arrive in force. It would not be unusual for it to be raining long before New Year.

We have a three-hour boat trip cruising down half the gorge, before crossing a rocky outcrop which divides it, and then transferring to a smaller boat on the other side. Taking seats on plastic chairs the staff provide bin liners in-lieu of waterproofs. The boat chugs down the gorge, and the young guide talks us through. We disembark and walk over a rocky, slippery rock to where the gorge continues and board a smaller, uncovered boat.

"You're all going to get wet!" remarks the guide, taking his position at the wheel once more.

We motor through small passages and inlets in the side of the gorge. On the way back, the guide allows a trio of schoolboys a turn on the wheel each, so the course we take is a meandering one. A group of canoeists struggle to manhandle their canoes over the rocky outcrop. I turn to the guide and say:

"No wonder you blokes couldn't handle Gallipoli!"

At the boat ramp, Anna and Klaus get talking to two English girls who turn up in the next party who recognise them. They are wearing nothing but bikinis and thongs, and rain jackets over their shoulders. One comes from Ealing, west London, and the other comes from Northwood.

Klaus cooks a fantastic Thai Green Chicken Curry, and we have it outside on the table with candles and wine. Georgina serves up Mango she has bought and demonstrates how to eat it; you cut the fruit in half, and score criss-cross lines through one half. Inverting the fruit, and pushing the fruit upwards, the sections splay ready to eat.

The rain has not let up. We head out to natural springs, where warm water gushes up from the ground and fills a shallow stream. We strip off and wallow in the pleasant, clear water. Back at the car, the last few overs of the final fifth Test from the Sydney Cricket Ground is being broadcast, and England are on the verge of a well-deserved–and belated victory as Australia are 220 for 8, or as the Australians put it, 8 for 220. As I sit in the driver's seat and wait for the others, England win by 225 runs.

We head back to the accommodation, stopping at Red Rooster for lunch. We spend the rest of the day moping around, unwilling to do much because of the weather.

I get an SMS from Dave telling me he left Perth on New Year's Eve, and that meeting a Swiss-Italian girl on the Indian Pacific that night, travelled with her to Adelaide and on to Melbourne.

Anna has an unused portion of her bus ticket she wants to

use, so she leaves that night for Alice, where we will meet her. The rain gets heavier and heavier until the cars are squeaky clean and shiny, and the pits in the road are full of water, and the gutters are overflowing.

Driving Day 8: Katherine – Tennant Creek

The day is grim, and it is still raining lightly when we get up and check out.

Timber Creek, our halfway point on our way to Alice Springs. It is just too far to drive from Katherine to Alice in one day, but the journey splits in to two legs. The main highway is the Stuart Highway, which passes along the site of the old Telegraph line constructed from Darwin to Adelaide. We pass Mataranka, home to a well-known thermal pool, and the site of what is believed to be the world's largest anthill.

Georgina and I stop at a roadhouse where the restaurant and bar are upstairs alongside a veranda and find Klaus having breakfast there. I fancy a change of car, so I get in the passenger seat next to Klaus. Powderfinger's album *Odyssey Number Five* plays on the old car stereo. Klaus has an easy-going intelligence, mature deposition, and his English is nigh on perfect making him a good travel companion. By lunchtime, the skies clear, and the temperature rises, and the sun emerges.

Renner Springs is our next roadhouse stop, well known for the hundreds of caps, memorabilia and personal items left pinned to the roof of the bar by hundreds of travellers passing through.

Our last stop for the day, Tennant Creek, is a medium-sized town between Alice and Katherine, not far from the turnoff for the main highway running west-east to Townsville, and therefore a strategic supply town in outback Northern Territory. The site was dictated by the breakdown of a beer truck destined for a pub construction site at the Overland Telegraph station ten kilometres distant. Rather than haul the truck's cargo the rest of the way, it was decided to build the town where the truck had halted.

We find a hostel run by an Englishman from the North of England. Klaus and I are dying for a good feed, so we head over to a new club across the road and order hamburger and chips, washed down by schooners of beer. I inspect a fishing board listing the recent catches in the district. Anna's bus is due into town early, whilst many of us are still sleeping.

Driving Day 9: The Alice

On our final leg to Alice, we visit the Devil's Marbles, a huge collection of spherical, rocky, boulders, spread out over several kilometres off the main highway. We attempt to climb a few, and by stretching to the limits of our arms, on our tiptoes, we can just about climb to the top.

We stop at Wycliffe Well, a famous roadhouse and area renowned for UFO sightings. A local developer has created an artificial crayfish fishing area. A huge exhibition in the servo covers the UFO sightings, and a self-congratulatory display charts the resort construction.

I bump into the two girls we met at the mooring ramp at Katherine Gorge and get chatting. The entire group are unhappy with their guide and driver, who is grumpy and unhelpful; certainly not the usual charismatic local usually encountered in the tourist industry over here.

Our last roadhouse on the way in to Alice is Aileron, and we stop for a milkshake and fruit. Out the front is a group of lads unloading a Commodore ute with slabs of soft drinks, probably carted in from Alice.

***

Alice Springs is a service town in the middle of the continent. For some reason, people travelling there connect Alice with Ayers Rock. Surely one is only a few miles from the other?— the reality is Uluru is still a good four-hour drive away. We have agreed to meet Klaus at Toddy's resort.

Klaus pulls up at the front: I wave him in, and he swings madly around the forecourt, pulling into a spare bay. He stops too close to a spiral staircase, and a step smashes his offside headlight in a tinkle of broken glass. Klaus shakes his head in a stupor of fatigue.

That evening, the girls are in the room, and Klaus and I sit at the bar and talk to an easy-going, blonde Australian barmaid with short hair, who has recently moved to Alice from Melbourne. She is working for a services company in Alice, bolstering her income by working behind the bar in the evenings. The bar's operation is simple; on the floor behind the counter, a huge esky containing tinnies of beer; above the bar, seven or eight empty cans are screwed to a wooden plinth, so visitors know what is on offer.

Klaus and I start with our favourites and move along the line trying new lines. We finish both Victoria Bitter and Melbourne Bitter—same brewery—try Hahn lite, Fosters, Castlemaine XXXX, Swan, Emu and Tooheys. By this stage, the beer tastes the same, and we are worse for wear. The barmaid talks about Melbourne, and the footy there, and complains about her job installing air-conditioners in hospitals. We sympathise through an alcoholic haze. The tinnies get scrunched up and thrown on to the heap we've amassed.

***

Uluru is next. But first, a stop at a breaker's yard, where we buy and fit a replacement headlight for Klaus's Ford and an indicator light.

We head south out of town, following the Stuart Highway south and turn. After travelling west for an hour, we stop off at a rest-spot. We sight Mount Connor, otherwise known as the "false rock", as it is often mistaken for Uluru by travellers. Half an hour, later the Rock itself comes into view, and never leaves our sight. It's impressive, even from this distance.

The campsite at the Uluru Tourist Resort is 30 minutes from the Rock. We find a patch of grass near the kitchen and ablution blocks, and pitch our tent and luxuriate in the AC of the reception area. We jump in the pool and revel in the water. Nearing sunset, we walk along a wooden catwalk leading out over the bush to a viewing area and watch the sun go down, our figures casting long shadows over the bush for many metres.

Georgina is going to sleep on the grass in her sleeping bag, and Klaus and Anna are going to share the small tent. I don't fancy getting bitten to death in the grass, so fall asleep in one of Klaus's chairs. Before I nod off, I watch the sky and the stars and listen to the noises of the campsite. In the moonlight, tens of rabbits come out and play, chasing each other across the lawn where we have pitched our tents. They venture close to me but scamper away when I shift.

The Rock. It's a 4.30am start for us, heralded by a lightening in the sky. Klaus drives towards Uluru, as the sky turns different colours. It is the only distinguishable feature in the distance, and as the road winds towards it, we appear to get closer, but then further away, by turns. We halt near a ragtag melee of cars, coaches and minibuses parked by the side of the road at a sunrise viewing area. It is now dawn. The sun lurches above the desert horizon sometime after.

When the sun breaches the line on schedule, everyone is ready, and there are "oohs" and "ahs" as the first of the sun's rays project on to the rock. We hear hundreds of muted camera-captures, as people chart the course of the sun's ray's progress up the rock, watching the changing colours.

We will walk clockwise around Uluru starting in the shade, finishing in the sun. We find the path follows the rock closely, and the rock is surrounded by groups of fertile trees and flora and fauna which provides shade. I grab a towel and drape it around my shoulders to ward off the sun's rays.

There are several little attractions and distractions; walkways disappear into a fissure or crack in the rock, where Aboriginal art or artefacts can be found on the rocky overhangs, or where spirits would be found. There are also sacred areas, where only aboriginal women or men can congregate—out of bounds to visitors. The Aboriginal writers in the guide ask tourists to respect their culture. Any tourists considering desecrating any of Uluru could be prosecuted under "Cultural" legislation that exists under Australian law.

At the halfway point, we arrive at the main car park, and the section of the rock where tourists may climb, if they wish to do so. It is not an easy task. The initial section is so steep anyone failing to hang on to the rope, or slips, would probably roll back in to the carpark. As today's temperature is going to rise above 40 degrees, the climb is closed. (High winds would also close the climb.)

By the time we get to the other side of the rock, the sun has climbed higher, and we come out from the relative shade of the western side into the morning heat. Both Anna and Georgina are struggling, so I give my towel to Georgina to cover her head with, and I take Anna's backpack from her.

The car interior is super-heated, and by the time we arrive at the visitor's centre, we are glad to buy cold drinks. The long drive back to Alice is unbearable, but it's even worse in the back. The four-hour journey seems interminable, and when we arrive back at Toddy's, I'm crying out for a cold one. Wasting no time, I strip off and jump in the pool, enjoying the cool water.

We have our last meal together as Klaus and Anna are leaving. I cook Georgina a meal of Spaghetti Bolognaise, and we sit outside the room. I am tucking into this when I become am aware of a tickling sensation on my thigh. I glance down and to my horror, see a Huntsman spider advancing towards my shorts. I spring up, allowing it to fall on to the concrete and scurry away to the wall, where it sits for the rest of the evening. They are not poisonous but can nonetheless deliver a painful bite.

Georgina and I say goodbye to Klaus and Anna; she is getting on a bus to Coober Pedy and then on to Melbourne by the Great Ocean Road.

***

BLING. I get an SMS from the aeroplane boys telling us of their imminent arrival in Alice—they arrive this evening, so I tell them to come to Toddy's. I go over to reception and book them beds in our room. There is a knock on the door of the room, and I open it to see Rich and Colin standing outside beaming. The Suzuki is covered in fine, red dust, and Rich tells us the story:

They left Perth after New Year's Day and sped to Kalgoorlie along the well-paved highway then headed to Esperance on the south coast. During an evening stopover, they came up with the madcap plan of driving off-road along dirt tracks across the middle of Western Australia directly to Alice to meet up with us. All things were going well, but they got a puncture and had to backtrack several hundred kilometres on the spare to get another, which involved a day's wait whilst the local garage got the replacement in.

"But you've got a 4x4. It's not as if you were doing the trip in a Ford or Holden," I say.

"Yeah, but it's different for a small 4x4," replies Colin. Larger 4x4s travelling at speeds of about 60 or 70 miles per hour pack the dirt road in to corrugations, and vehicles can skim across these with a rhythmic hum. The small wheelbase Suzuki had problems riding out the corrugations, so it was a bumpy ride.

"What happened to my old mate Dave in Perth?" I ask.

Dave left Perth on New Year's Eve, catching the Indian Pacific train east back through Adelaide aiming for Sydney. I tell the boys what I know; that he met a Swiss-Italian girl on the train and travelled on down to Melbourne with a group of people in a hired camper van. We head over to the pub to catch up.

***

I hike down to Alice Springs station to catch the southbound Ghan train to Adelaide, the start of my trip back towards the East Coast and "home".

After checking in my rucksack, I bump into Brett, who is serving behind the buffet.

"How's Rebecca, mate?" I ask, remembering her from Adelaide.

His expression changes—she has just left and returned to the UK only days before.

"Catch you in a tick."

In his break, he comes and sits down, chucking a Mars bar from the buffet in to my lap. We catch up. He is morose about Rebecca. He is interested in flying as he is looking for something else to do after his current stint as a steward.

"Tell you what–come and stay with us for a bit. We'll show you around," he offers. "The boys won't mind."

On arrival, I collect my rucksack from the baggage cart and stand in the carpark waiting for him. Brett calls me over, and we walk to the carpark reserved for railway staff and get into an old Mitsubishi Sigma belonging to his flatmate, Marty, who also works on the railways. Jason, another young lad from the train —who was in Gold Kangaroo service, aged about 23, also comes with us. He made good tips last night.

Brett's Sigma runs out of gas, and we have barely coasted to a halt when Brett whips a petrol can out of the back of the car. After tipping the contents into the tank, there are annoying seconds while the engine refuses to start, but soon we're filling up a hundred metres down the road at the next servo. We are hungry—I haven't eaten since lunchtime yesterday, and so we head over to MacDonalds for a feed before returning to their house. Hanging around with Marty, Jason and Brett: days of fast-paced drinking, partying and hanging out beckons.

***

Brett and Marty share a run-down bungalow in a suburb not far from the station, with car-parking out front. They have a communal pool in the front garden, but a man living in the nearest bungalow treats it like it's his. The house is a bloke's dream—equipped with PC, DVD player, Play Station 2, video, TV, cinema amp with subwoofer, all belonging to Brett.

"But I'd sell all this rubbish tomorrow, Steve," he tells me, "if it means I could go over to England to be with Rebecca."

A pub across the road advertises a quiz night, so we head over. Some questions need local knowledge:

What was the name of the Queen of England who reigned for only nine days?

[The answer is of course Lady Jane Grey—sixteenth century.]

"I knew we'd get one of the answers out of you," Brett says.

We discuss plans before my train leaves for Sydney on Saturday. I mention it will be my 30th birthday on Sunday. Brett's eyes light up, and he exchanges a look with Jason.

"The Schutzenfest!" they say in unison.

It's a German beer festival that comes to Adelaide annually.

"Stay Saturday night, and get the Sunday train–I'll get you an upgrade to Silver service," Brett says.

Brett and I hang around winding down the clock. There are a lot of photos of Rebecca around. He is upset and puzzled over their split up. I take a liking to Brett, to his honesty and friendship. He talks to me about his time in the Navy and his overseas trips to the United States and London. When he was serving in the Persian Gulf, during the liberation of Kuwait in '91, he was shot in the chest by an Iraqi whilst his section was carrying out a routine ship boarding, and he spent weeks recovering in hospital. The only testament is a small scar on his chest.

"Did it hurt, Brett?" I ask.

"It was like this," Brett says, and burrows his index finger in to my chest as hard as he can.

He's not the only guy whose relationship has unravelled—Jason turns up announcing he has split up from his girlfriend.

***

The day of the Schutzenfest is warm, and we know it is going to be a stinking hot South Australian day. T-shirts and shorts, and sunblock is the order of the day. We get a lift over with a friend who came over the night before and ended up staying the night.

A series of tents have been erected on the grass. Brett is low on cash, so I shout a beer stein each from a tent, and thus equipped, stop at one of the beer stops and buy foaming pints of beer. Sipping them, we make circuits around the ground before settling on a beer tent in the middle. We stand—all the tables are full—amongst parties of drinkers, laughing and joking and throwing inflatable balls around at each other. Brett has a term for an attractive girl—a "giddy up" girl and he points out several walking around. Jason turns up with the girlfriend he has just split up from, Heidi, and a friend of hers.

Afternoon arrives. There are a fair few people here, and everyone stands around watching everyone else. I can see a police presence here, and we watch two policewomen escort a youth away for spraying revellers in a tent with a large water pistol, citing a public order offence. Onlookers watch. Brett and I talk to the girls—they are fun and talkative.

The rest of the afternoon passes by in a blur—the crowds get bigger and bigger; the temperature drops a mite. There is a moment of hostility when friends of Heidi turn up and are abusive to Jason, and Brett, ever the diplomat—ever the honest broker—calms things down.

Back at the house, with the light fading, we decide to risk the wrath of Brett's neighbour and go for a swim in the pool. As midnight approaches, I announce the imminent passing of another decade. Moments later, Brett makes a clumsy pass at Heidi's friend and Jason gets mad at Brett, and the two start a massive full-on "blue" (an Australian word for an argument.) The two girls and boys scream at each other. So—as the stroke of midnight passes—I stand in the garden alone and shake my head at their antics.

***

On the weekend, Brett offers to take us back to the station so I can return to Sydney. He's pulled a few strings with the railway, and I find I have been upgraded to Silver Service. In this increased luxury, I start a paperback I find discarded in the buffet car—Nick Hornby's *About a Boy*.

I get talking to three English girls in the lounge car. One is a Kylie Minogue look-a-like, a trainee podiatrist from the south of England. The second is a dark-haired girl from Kent, who reminds me of a cross between a character from *Brookside* and Posh Spice. Finally, a tall girl from the north of England. She always seems to wear an expression of boredom.

We get off the train in Broken Hill, and endure the heat walking to the Musicians Club, on Crystal Street. A sign tells us Broken Hill has the only legal school for the traditional military ANZAC (Australian New Zealand Army Corps) gambling "two-up" game in New South Wales. We enjoy a latte each—I ask for extra hot—before reboarding the train, resigning ourselves to the last leg.

The rest of the journey into Sydney, we play a game of Travel Monopoly, and the car fills up with children, so the girls and I find we've established a sort of creche and have an obligation to keep them entertained.

That night in Sydney, I go out with the girls, and when we get back to the hostel on Kent Street, we find a new arrival has checked in. He's a doctor from London, all kitted up with a brand-new rucksack complete with mesh wire security bag. One of the girls climbs into bed with him.

"Doctor, Doctor! I feel sick!" she says.

He tells her to get lost as he's getting up early in the morning to climb the Harbour Bridge.

Pilot Dave from London is now in Manly, a well-known beach on the north shore of the Harbour. I catch a ferry over, and the lauded beach comes in to view. I book in to the room next to his. Dave greets me, and after updating each other on the balcony outside our rooms, we go off and have a coffee in a hotel on a corner overlooking the esplanade. I stir my cappuccino, Dave favours a Big M ice-cold coffee.

I knew he had ended in Melbourne with a group of people, and it turns out they hired a camper van and drove there from Adelaide along the famous Great Ocean Road. There was a bit of pressure in the group, though, so he ended up leaving them in a seaside town and hiring a car to take him to Sydney.

"I got fed up with them, Steve," he says. "I wanted to camp, but they wanted a hostel."

Dave departs Sydney the next day to return to the UK—I'm sad to see him go, but I'm glad we got to fly together.

CHAPTER 23 A YEAR TO REMEMBER - AUSTRALIA DAY

Arriving back in Sydney for what seems like the umpteenth time, I realise that as I am due to fly back to the UK in a matter of days, I need to get organised. My cousin's toddler has started to talk in sentences and is going through a phase of asking for me by name. Happily, my cousin tells me Chris is expected down in the morning, and I have my head deep in the paper behind the reception desk at my cousin's office when Chris walks in on Thursday.

"G'Day Kippers!" he says.

I realise I haven't seen him since the Grand Final weekend in October. He thinks for a bit.

"Hey Kippers. What are you up to?"

"Not much," I reply.

"Tell you what," he says. "Come up. We're going over to the island on the river for Australia Day with my mate Riley in his boat. There's also a band on in the club on Saturday, and, the new tavern's open."

It sounds like too good an opportunity to miss, so I grab my gear.

Australia Day is an annual holiday observed by many Australians. It commemorates the anniversary of when the First Fleet arrived in Botany Bay over 200 years ago, and as it falls in high-summer, most Australians celebrate it by having a bar-b-que and friends over.

We head up the familiar highway towards South West Rocks. Down on the river, there is a newly completed tavern by the jetty. It's set back from the banks, with commanding views, and the island in the distance. We sit outside, enjoying the summer's evening.

On Saturday, Chris, as player-coach, is batting at a cricket match in Kempsey, so I go with him. We pull up in the carpark at the Country Club and find members of the team in the nets batting and bowling. The school-age boys are impressive at this level.

At the toss, Chris elects to bat first, and South West Rocks' opening batsmen partnership get their first runs on the board. The boys who are not batting ask me questions about England. Soon it is Chris's turn in the order. After watching him settle and turn a few balls away for safe runs, I get an ice-cream. I turn away only to hear a South West Rocks' wicket fall. Later, I see Chris sitting sheepishly under a tree.

"I thought you were batting, Chris," I ask, grinning.

"I was out for four Steve," he replies, grimacing with disgust.

Julie has been busy packing bedding, food and camping gear, so we load the car and we drive to the jetty in the Camry, fishing rods extending through the back windows.

Scanning the horizon in the approaching twilight, Riley can be seen in the distance approaching with his boats, a large cruiser with cabin, and a smaller fishing dingy towed alongside. He drifts alongside the jetty and throws me a line. Within minutes, Julie, Chris, Cassie and her school friend, and their puppy, are on board, and I am sitting in the bow deck with the rope.

"Hey Steve!" calls Riley through the window. "Stay up out on top. When we get there, I want you to throw out the anchor line."

We head out towards the mouth of the river, and Riley keeps over to the right hand, passing the new tavern. Chris's house is just visible atop the hill in the darkening light.

Soon the island comes in to view in the growing dusk. Our cabin can be seen from the jetty. Riley grabs a ladder out of a shed nearby and hangs it above the water so we can disembark and walk there in the dusk.

We scurry around in the dark, before Julie lights lanterns. The cabin is bare, and clad in timber like a Swiss ski chalet. The room has bunk beds and a large trestle picnic-style table and bench is centre stage. A curtain hides the master bedroom. The girls commandeer it and find a mirror for their make-up sessions.

Australia Day is the 26th: we are pleased to see friends turn up in their powerboat with the Sunday papers and food, and they hang around. Riley and I head out in his small boat to inspect and empty his crab traps.

"Watch out for the crab's claws," he warns me.

We motor down the river and turn in to a shallow inlet dappled with sunlight, just deep enough to take the boat's draught. Riley identifies a crab trap—I can just spot the outline under the surface. It is crate-sized, and we can see mud crabs caught inside. They have migrated to the highest corner of the trap, with claws and legs dangling outside.

He opens the trap and shakes out a crab. It is a good six inches across, and big enough to keep. He masterfully handles the crab: setting it down on the floor, he kneels and places his foot on its back. He gets a length of twine, and ties it up, before chucking it in to a bucket. There's a mass of crabs jostling and climbing over each other.

Back at the cabin, I pull a crab out of the bucket and set it down on the veranda, allowing it to scurry slowly along the floor towards the puppy, who watches it with great interest, sniffing it inquisitively. When the young girls come back, I dangle it in front of them, and they scream.

Riley drops the crabs in to a huge pot of boiling water and boils them for a good half an hour, their shells turning from dark green to bright orange. He pronounces them well cooked; and sitting astride the bench, barefooted, he fillets the crabmeat.

The boys and girls play a game of cricket on the neat-cropped grass next door to the cabin. We set up boxes for wickets, and with me installed as batsman, Chris runs up to bowl. I am determined to give a good account of myself as I know Chris will sledge me endlessly if I live up to expectations as an English cricketer.

"Watch this, Kippers," he crows. As an aside to the girls, he mutters, "He won't even hit it..."

The first ball comes arching through the air towards me and I realise I haven't picked up a bat in anger since I was aged 12 at secondary school. Somehow, I connect, and send the ball to the grass and gain my first run.

"Swings like a rusty gate," observes Chris.

"The gloves are off," pronounces Riley.

I find my line and length, and hit a brace of "sixes".

I mass a score of 13, before Riley bowls me. Chris bats, and I head over to the tree line, ready to field the inevitable high balls I know Chris will put up for me.

"Get ready, Kippers," he calls, as Riley bowls.

Chris swings expertly and sends a few balls in to the trees for "four", and we have to scamper around under boughs and roots to find the ball, while Chris stands at his crease and wipes his brow. I am pleased to get my fingers to a high ball and get him out.

A man and boys have turned up on the other side of the playing area, and have set up a tent, and when a stray ball crashes into their tent area, they obligingly return it, so Chris invites them to join in. As befits Australian boys, they are natural cricketers, with smooth actions. Less running for me now in the field, and I can position one of the boys in the sun, allowing myself the safety and luxury of the shade.

The young boys, about 11 or 12, look at the girls.

"There's girls here," I hear them mutter.

They choreograph their frequent troops past our cabin to go fishing to time with when Cassie and her friend perform cartwheels and acrobatics out in front.

At "drinks", Julie calls us over as she has spotted a goanna, also known as a sand monitor, in the grass outside the dunny. It is huge; the size of a small dachshund. They grow to five feet tall, including the tail, and resemble iguanas. It scurries up a tree, and we all gather around to watch it.

The new day is barely going when Chris comes up to me with a broad grin on his face:

"I've got a job for you, Kippers..." he says, as we tidy up for our departure. "You can empty the bucket in the dunny! We've all done it on past trips–you can do it this time."

To conclude my trip, Chris gives me a lift into Kempsey for the train, and we have lunch at the café he and Julie used to own. He drops me off at the station, and leaves, tooting his horn; I am sad to see him go.

***

I get back on a Saturday afternoon and can't face the thought of another night in a "party central" hostel with drunken backpackers, lights being turned on in the early hours, queues for showers, and the general bother. It's as if I want to get away from it all my final week back to adulthood. What's last on the menu?

A daytrip to the Blue Mountains, out west. The mountains are so named due to the blue haze that hangs in the air due to the eucalyptus leaves, and the spa town of Katoomba is the geographic heart. I board the train which arrives late in the afternoon. There has been a cold spell; the village is ensconced in a dark mist, and it is trying to spit with rain. The village looks Tyrolean; the buildings are older looking, and craggy, as befits a Victorian spa town.

I find the road leading to the hostel, a narrow and winding road with a narrow footpath. I am reminded of an English town in the Peak District or a village in North Wales, and glory in the cool climate. The hostel entrance is in an alleyway in the high street. The interior is cosy, sort of British B&B style. I check in and go downstairs to the common room, which is windy and cool, as someone has left the backdoor room open whilst they have a cigarette outside on the terrace.

I get talking to an occupational therapist, called Kirsty, who comes from Clapham, South London, and a nurse from South

Africa who has been working in London for the last few years. They talk about their experiences in hospitals, and Kirsty tells me about the drunkards in casualty on a Saturday night at Kingston Hospital I stayed in years back when I was admitted with suspected malaria.

I go upstairs and find a plush and formal dining room with a large tea urn on perpetual simmer. A man and a woman are having loud, boisterous sex in a room off it and a backpacker is sitting in the corner grinning. My room is small and square, and I occupy one of the top bunks, next to a window that looks out in to the bin area.

Kirsty has organised a riding trip with a stable nearby, so I tag along. We are picked up by a feral-looking man in an Akubra hat in an old Sigma. We wind our way through to Blackheath, and we can see the extent of the recent bushfires that raged through here weeks before. The trees beside the road are charred black.

We are the only two in this ride, and we are led out by a tall willowy rider for a three-hour rideout. We break into a trot down a section of path, and our leader turns around and says:

"That's a pretty good trot for a beginner." Kirsty helps me out:

"He was a jackeroo," she says.

"OK. No worries then," replies the leader.

Out on the flat, we get the chance to canter, a chance to review the skills used this year.

Back at the school, there is a large party of Americans who are waiting to be matched with steeds, and a girl making a fuss over the fact that she has been matched with a small pony.

"I don't want to ride that!" she says, pointing towards it.

She sounds like a spoilt brat, but I can see her point—it's more or less a Shetland. The ride leader gives us a lift back and points out a bend where she once lost control of her car. She ended up wedged in a clump of trees, overhanging the drop. She walked away unscathed.

The next day at breakfast, we have eggs and omelette served

on plates the size of dustbin lids. I grab the *Daily Telegraph* and see the space shuttle Columbia has disintegrated just before re-entry; the photos are all over the front pages of the daily newspapers. I say goodbye to Kirsty.

The next morning will herald my last day in Australia, after a year away.

I head with a French girl to Coogee and splash around in the surf, and much to my dismay, walking back along Coogee Bay Road, I realise I have caught a touch of sunburn. For my last night in Sydney, I am back where I stayed when I first arrived —which seems kind of fitting. I am feeling dehydrated from the beach, and she is not feeling so good, so we decide to have a night in.

My new French friend shows me her sunburn standing on tiptoe, calf and thigh muscles stretched, examining the backs of her legs in the mirror on the dorm door.

I walk down to the beach at sunset past the late-evening revellers and sit for a while looking out to sea, collecting my thoughts—it's the end of summer for me, and back to a winter in the UK.

Last day—London is on my mind—but we visit the Rocks next to Circular Quay stopping at a sports coffee shop owned by David Campese, a famous Australian rugby player (101 appearances at international level.) He is behind the counter today, and I buy a new blue "home" New South Wales Waratahs top to replace the white "away" one I have practically worn out this year. With hours to go before my flight departs, we sprint for the 273 bus back to Coogee, and I head to the airport.

There is one final drama to come. Remember the slight delay in Dubai when the groundstaff couldn't find my visa? My working visa didn't flag in the computer due to a swap of an "8" and "A" in my passport. It turns out the attendant issued me with a three-month visa there and then without telling me. I have overstayed on this visa and so get a ban from Australia for two years. My working visa? it's unused and will expire soon anyhow.

"The embassy in London will sort it," says the ground staff.

Armed with this reassuring knowledge, my flight takes off on-time toward Singapore.

PHOTOS AND OTHER BOOKS
A Year On Land and Sea (Amazon)

Have you ever danced with the devil and parachuted in the moonlight? Juggled work with play? Tried to keep a romance alive whilst working as a swordsman on a Hollywood movie set? In 1995, Steve was trying to figure out how to take a degree in London, keep up with his military training, and learn to sail. A trip across the Atlantic to the Caribbean and island cruising was just the ticket. Will he learn to sail, pass his exam, get to the Tropics, keep his girlfriend happy, or will he end up in the doldrums?

stephenmalinsauthor.com (Photos)

Reflections (2002 & 2020) from the author:

A final thought (2002)

I land at Heathrow to discover London is still gripped and subdued by winter, seemingly unchanged since I left it the year before. Had summer ever arrived? The sky seems considerably lower than "down under", and it seems dark even at mid-morning. On the flight, I was able to reflect a bit. I got a real insight to the Australia that perhaps many travellers or tourists don't see—the regions not the more travelled cities and coast. It is without a doubt a country of contrasts, a hedonistic modern western country but by shades backward, and out-of-date, but nonetheless perhaps the more charming for it. For example, parts of Western Australia are completely isolated: Perth is a case in point. The pace of life is perceived to be somewhat faster, and optimal on the East Coast, and few cities can match the climate and natural beauty of Sydney Harbour.

It seems to me many English people expect Australia to be "England in the Sun", and whilst the country retains an Anglo-Saxon outlook in humour, culture and conversation, much of the convenience and physical attributes of the media, housing, stores, streets and cars owe more to the influences of North America. Despite this Americanisation, there is still an European, Anglo (and Asian) influence where the national attitude is very much "She'll be alright", and where the national catchphrase is still "No worries". And in a continent so far from American and European shores, there is no doubt that Australia's trading future is with Asia and so Singapore and China will play an important role in future, more so than say, England, Italy or Greece.

Most visitors to Australia find the people laid-back and friendly. Much has been made of the Australian cultural phenomenon of sport, bbq, sense of "fair play" and gender stereotypes; until very recently the Australian male was lampooned as a sexist, beer swilling, footie-watching ocker, dressed in singlet, shorts and thongs who baited the "Sheilas";

feisty, chirpy, confident woman who could give as well as take. Paul Hogan and Crocodile Dundee did much to bolster this image in the 1980s. In the country, to an extent, this stereotype is alive and well amongst the farmers and miners from Queensland to Western Australia. It is still certainly the case informal segregation is still practised at bar-b-ques. The people have developed a brand of confidence and independence which is second to none in the UK or the US. And the cities are vibrant, multi-cultural and modern.

Undoubtedly, this national character is shaped very much by the climate. The weather is largely fine throughout the year, without the weeks of overcast days or days of drizzle typical in the northern hemisphere, apart from cooler days and rapid cooling at night in the southern latitudes in the winter, and the "Wet" in the tropical north. The sun shines most of the time, and days of rain soon pass. This clearly does not deter the thousands of immigrants who arrive in Australia hoping to start a new life. Since the 1950s, thousands of migrants have arrived from Greece and Italy. A well-publicised programme during that time was British people, known as "ten-pound Pom's", paying just ten pounds for the privilege. But Australia has its own problems with drugs, illegal immigration, and the unsolved legacy of the indigenous population, as I witnessed myself in the large Aboriginal population centres of Katherine and Alice Springs in the Northern Territory.

Whilst Australia operates a strict system of migration, and welcomes skilled entry, the problem with illegal immigrants and refugees has been the subject of great focus, and, many more people gain entry illegally, particularly boat people from Asia. The Commonwealth Government takes this very seriously, and many end up at Woomera, a prison-camp facility in the South Australian desert. But it is still worthwhile for people to try; there were shocking claims in early 2001 of boat people throwing their children into the sea off Queensland, hoping to be taken on board by Australian Navy ships. This was used cynically by John Howard's government as an election ploy in their late 2001 re-election.

On balance, Australia has spoils and riches available to those that can make the most of them, and it rewards those who work hard, as the original colonists found to their gain.

A final thought (2020)

England lost their Rugby Grand slam in 2002, but went on to win the Six Nations Grand Slam the next year in 2003, the first clean sweep since 1995. That year was a lucky one—for at the end of it, in November, in Sydney, at Stadium Australia, England's Johnny Wilkinson kicked a drop goal to win the World Cup against Australia 20-17 after extra time.

"You haven't mentioned it yet!" says Chris, the next time I see him, when I return to Australia with my wife to be in 2004:

"Water off a duck's back, mate!" I reply.

ACKNOWLEDGEMENT

I'd like to thank Simon Michael Prior, Alison Ripley-Cubitt and Liza Grantham for their assistance with my manuscript, and all those who can't be, (or would rather not be) named for their kind encouragement. Also to my darling wife Kiki, and children, who put up with my excitement as the book took shape some 20 years after events and since I first put pen to paper in 2003.

ABOUT THE AUTHOR

Stephen M Malins

Years later, Steve now lives in Melbourne with his wife, and three teenagers. He is an unpaid uber driver for his many sins.

He still works in IT (it seems nothing has changed), but volunteered as a Country Fire Authority firefighter and loves getting out in the High Country and on skis in the Australian Alps.

Printed in Great Britain
by Amazon